HOW TO RESTORE YOUR COLLECTOR

Bicycle

WILLIAM LOVE

WAM
books

First Published in 2001 by MBI
Publishing Company, St. Paul, MN
55101 USA

Second printing Published in 2009 by
WAM Books, Spokane, WA 99203
USA

Printed in United States of America

ISBN 978-0-615-28243-5

Edited by Steve Hendrickson
Designed by Dan Perry

On the front cover:
The 1954 Schwinn Black Phantom was
a favorite bike of kids in the 1950s, and
it's a favorite among collectors and
restorers today. Excellent original or
restored Phantoms sell for thousands of
dollars, but restoring one isn't much
more difficult than any other old bike.
Jeff Hackett

Insets:
Here is the author at work
disassembling and restoring some 1960s
vintage Schwinn middleweight bikes.

On the back cover:
After purchasing the Excelsior
Motorcycle Company, Schwinn used
the Excelsior name on its bicycle
badges. High quality details, such as
this badge on a 1950 Red Phantom, are
part of the reason these bikes are so
sought after today.

This beautifully restored 1948 J.C.
Higgins uses the original color scheme.
The skirt guards "stolen" from a girl's
model add a nice touch.

CONTENTS

Ever since I was a kid, bicycles have occupied a part of my life. One thing I have learned while writing this book is that I am certainly not alone in this. Many of us share this interest and admiration of bicycles to some degree, from casual to downright eccentric.

In my research for this book, I contacted several people, who, like myself, happily occupy the eccentric end of the scale. I want to thank all of these people for their help during the process of assembling this work. They were all generous with their time, information, and the sharing of their collections for photos.

I acknowledge and thank these individuals in alphabetical order by last name:

Greg Bacha describes himself as a detail man, which I can identify with. He's probably a bit of a perfectionist too. As soon as he gets a bike, he does research to be sure that he has all of the stock or original parts to make it right. Greg favors Schwinn Sting-Rays and other early 20-inch bicycles.

Kathy Bruce has practically been raised in a bicycle shop. Her dad opened Columbia Cycle and Hobby in 1952. Bruce was born quite a bit later but now runs the store. A branch of her "bicycle life" is Columbia Cycle Classics. Bruce's collection consists of hundreds of vintage bikes, so I guess she must like them.

Mike Carver likes originality in his vintage bikes. He is even able to recount a story involving a fender dent that was pounded out by a nervous sister on her brother's new bike. It's Carver's bike now, but the 50-year-old story stays with it. Carver appreciates the early blending of motors and bicycles, so Whizzers fascinate him also.

Eric Christensen likes most old things, especially things he can make like new or improve via restoration and customizing. Christensen is a master automotive craftsman and painter. He produces show-winning rods and outstanding finishes on autos and bicycles. Christensen's bicycle interest is like many; he appreciates the collectibility and functionality of the old bikes, so he enjoys riding them as well as restoring them.

Cory Hayes owns a business in Spokane, Washington, called Master Blasters. His specialty is metal stripping, using many varieties of sand and other media for non-destructive paint and rust removal.

Jim Houghton demonstrates that there are bike "nuts" everywhere: between him and me, there are at least two just on our block. Houghton is my neighbor, and likes old cars, motorcycles, boats, and bicycles. Houghton built the "super bike" featured in chapter 9, and collects original vintage bikes as well.

Willard Stockton officially likes heavyweight J.C. Higgins bicycles. When he spots a good middleweight, however, or even a brand like Schwinn, it will show up in his garage. Stockton is the "guy with the fender roller," who regularly rolls (straightens) fenders for dozens of local collectors. He is happiest if he gets paid for this service with a part that he needs or a nifty accessory.

Stockton also has a nice collection of add-on accessories.

Dave Stromberger has liked heavyweight bikes for a long while. You can tell, because it takes awhile to collect the parts that fill his workshop. Stromberger's restorations have been so noticed that he is now restoring beautiful old heavyweights for other collectors. Since Stromberger puts so much time into total restoration, the very rare models are what he looks for.

Jerry Turner has an eye for the past as evidenced by the name of his business, Nostalgic Reflections. Turner has many old things in his total collection, including bikes, trucks, buses, cars, motorcycles, and bicycle head badges. Turner is a master fabricator, who can make about anything for everything, and vice versa. For our purposes, however, head badges and decals are his areas of expertise.

The entire staff at Super Color Photo, in Spokane, Washington, was dependable and accurate. Thanks to each individual for his/her help.

Mary Ann Love provided invaluable assistance during photography sessions. Hilary Love helped out with some of the photos, too, and both of them put up with my moody behavior while I assembled this book. Also thanks to Adam Love for some necessary computer instruction.

A final "thank you" to the Motorbooks International staff and others who helped bring this book to your shelf; Steve Hendrickson, Jane Mausser, the design staff, and Charles Pelkey formed a helpful, open, and responsive team.

Have you ever owned a bicycle? Very few of us can answer "no" to that question. Probably most of us can remember a favorite bicycle from our childhood. That special bike might have been yours, or one that belonged to a sibling, a friend, or a neighbor. Maybe it was displayed in the window of the local hobby shop and caught your eye.

For sure, the vibrant colors, sparkling chrome, fresh rubber, and dazzling accessories will always make bicycles have a captivating allure to kids as well as adults.

Bicycles hold a significant position in our past and present culture, and this stronghold is likely to continue for years to come. While "new and improved" versions capture our attention, bicycles of our past seem to stir our emotions and interest the most. When any product is manufactured with the philosophy of offering quality, function, and innovative design, a timeless appeal is often the result. Products meeting these tangible qualities somehow take on an intangible mystique, which leads to collectibility. Bicycles from myriad manufacturers and brands fall into this collectible category. They not only withstand the test of time physically, but most bicycles also have the functional and aesthetic qualities (design, color, accessories, and manufacturer history) that make them desirable to have, hold, and behold.

Collecting of all types is ever popular, and those who do so today may have found that the pastime has taken some new directions. Collectors

(of anything) in the past have most treasured pristine or fully restored examples of their particular passion. It is true that perfect original examples of an item still set the highest standard for value. It is in the "restored" category, however, where there has been some change in collectible standards. Restoration, or a newer term "over restoration," can actually lower the value of many collectibles. Antique furniture from the eighteenth and nineteenth centuries, for example, can lose over half its value by undergoing the previously popular stripping and refinishing. While some reconditioning of a good original piece may be in order, care must be taken to preserve and capture its original "patina."

Full, meticulous, perfect restoration is still an option for certain things (an extremely rare auto, toy, or bicycle), but few of us have the ability for such an undertaking. So, a major question in your selection and restoration of a bicycle will be: to paint or not to paint? Don't rule out painting a worthy collector bicycle, but read chapter 7 before you jump into such a project. The key is to either paint it right or preserve the original finish. This is where choosing the "right" collectible (one with the best combination of rarity, originality, and completeness) comes in. When you know what to look for, collecting bicycles that can be mechanically reconditioned while preserving their originality is quite satisfying. This area of collecting is the least taxing (once the item is found), most fun, and economically sound (few fully

restored items ever recapture the cost of restoration).

Among the most prized collector cars today are the "nostalgia" or "retro" hot rods. These are rods of the 1950s in their original "as used" condition, or ones that have been built today in the early genre. Bicycles follow this same trend. A good original bicycle from the 1950s or 1960s may have a few wear spots, or even some non-original accessories from the era, but will make a terrific collectible that you can use. Finding the bike, restoring it, and even riding it can be a very pleasant endeavor.

Collecting has many aspects. Locating, evaluating desirability, condition grading, and restoration are a few of these aspects, but pure enjoyment is the one that keeps the hobby going strong. Bicycles have all the qualities to make collecting them challenging and fun!

The following pages will guide you through bicycle restoration and more. Read this book from start to finish before you begin a restoration project. Whether you are just being introduced to the bicycle collector hobby, or you are an "old pro," the content is meant to be informative and enjoyable to you. The information is compiled from the real world experiences of bicycle collectors and restorers.

Hopefully, the chapters ahead will enhance your enjoyment of these two-wheeled vintage treasures and uncover new aspects of their collection and restoration. Look at the photos closely, as they will often tell a story beyond the scope of the caption. Have fun!

CHAPTER 1

Finding and Evaluating a Bicycle

Bicycle collectors are as varied as the bikes they collect. Some have hundreds, or even thousands of bikes, while others are content with one or two. Since bicycles have been produced for well over a hundred years, there are collectors who favor models from certain decades and those who covet specific brands.

For all of these hobbyists, collecting probably began with one special bicycle. This special bike might be one like they rode as a child, or even their actual childhood bike, rediscovered later in the parents' basement. For some collectors, it is a bike that they admired as a child but could never talk their parents into buying.

Since you are reading this book, you must either already have or are seeking that bike which is special to you. If you already have one or more bicycles, you can improve their mechanical and cosmetic condition via restoration. History shows that if you now have one or two collector bikes, you will eventually add to that number. Whether you are looking for your first collector bicycle, already

have one you wish to restore, or want to add to your collection, there are some considerations to ponder.

Bicycles have been around for a very long time. They began as walking machines in the early 1800s, and evolved through various designs, like

the high-wheeled Penny Farthings of the mid- to late-nineteenth century. By the 1890s, the new "safety" bicycle included most of today's features, such as two same-size wheels, a chain drive, and pneumatic tires. Sears & Roebuck had bikes in their catalogs

Sears marketed this model called the Master in about 1915. It is a true antique, and quite collectible, but its remaining numbers are too few to be in the collecting mainstream. It takes a lot of experience and expertise to restore bikes like this.

It's still quite old, but at least you can find parts for this 1938 Wards Hawthorne. It needs handlebars, a rear rack, and a chain guard, along with small items such as reflectors, handgrips, and pedals. This bike has several coats of bad paint, so Eric Christensen will do a sandblast and repaint (chapter 7).

before the widespread use of automobiles or electricity. In the 1908 catalog, five makes are represented: Elgin, Kenwood, Napoleon, Peerless, and Josephine. If you wanted a headlamp then, it was operated by kerosene or gas (calcium carbide). While these ancient bikes are true antiques, and certainly have collectible interest, their remaining numbers are too few to warrant discussion in detail here. Prime examples of the early relics are found mainly in museums, and can have values 15 to 20 times that of a 1950s balloon tire model.

The collectible bicycles of current mass interest are those from the decades of the 1930s through the 1970s. This group includes the popular balloon tire heavyweights, middleweights, Sting-Rays or muscle bikes, and even certain British and lightweight models.

The classic competition or racing bikes made during these same decades enthrall a large group of loyal fans. One reason for this is the fine engineering and construction evident on these models. These bikes incorporate super-high-quality components, like Campagnolo running gear, in their design. Racing-type bikes did not sell in quantity to the mass consumer market, so the current supply of these gems is not high but prices are.

If you already have a bike you wish to restore, part of your work is done, except you'll probably want more, once you have the collecting "bug." To find an old bike (your first, or an addition), there are several sources that can prove fruitful with a little effort and persistence. Most newspapers have a bicycle category in their classified section. When using this resource, be diligent. You need to check the ads daily, and the earlier, the better. These old bikes are getting scarcer all the time, so you must be the first to respond to an ad. Yard sales are a common place to find old bikes, but again, since the numbers of older bicycles are dwindling, go shopping *early*.

Contact bicycle shops and bicycle clubs in your area for available

Generally, the newer they are, the better condition they're in when you find them. This late 1950s Schwinn Jaguar Mark II is loaded with equipment, complete and original.

bikes. This word-of-mouth method, through the network of hobbyists, is a great way to gain information, as well as find bikes and parts. These clubs occasionally hold bicycle swap meets, which are a terrific place to look for what you want. Even automobile swap meets usually have some bicycle vendors in attendance. And guess what? That's right—get there early for the best finds.

Antique stores, pawnshops, and thrift stores (like Salvation Army) always have some bikes in stock. Late winter to early spring is the best time to find one. By midsummer they're usually all gone. You'll probably pay the most for a collector

bicycle at an antique store, but try to negotiate for the best price there or wherever you buy.

Bicycles, like everything else nowadays, are also available via the Internet. Online auction companies like eBay.com and Amazon.com regularly list hundreds of bikes at a time. Message boards, private and corporate website classifieds, and newsgroups all have areas specializing in collector bicycles. There are even whole UseNet newsgroups devoted to the trading and selling of classic bikes, parts, and accessories. The number of these sources you tap into is only limited by the time you want to spend at a computer. Chapter 10

lists some websites to get started with, but the Internet search engines list thousands of pages related to collector bicycles.

Bicycle collecting is not an exact science, with specific rules to follow. There are certain patterns or trends within the hobby, however, that can help guide you. Desirability of the various makes and models is somewhat a matter of personal taste, but the activity in the marketplace gives us some ideas to help us make judgments. Let's go over some of these general patterns now, and get more specific in chapter 2. Remember— the market trends discussed always have exceptions.

Most often, a boy's bike is more collectible than a girl's bike. Part of this is because of style (the high bar is a preferable aesthetic design), and part is plain old scarcity. It seems that boys must treat their bikes a bit rougher than girls do, because it's easier to find a girl's bike in excellent condition. The high frame bar on a boy's bike creates a good place for a tank/horn/light assembly, although many girls' bikes are equipped with tanks also. Some bikes are considered "loaded" from the factory, while others are quite plain. The fully equipped (tank, horn, light, rack, spring fork, etc.) model is usually more sought after than the basic model. Special factory equipment, however, is commonly missing from an old bike, and difficult to find. Basic models can benefit from add-on accessories (see chapter 9) to spruce them up. Certain collectors specialize in basic models, though, so there are no absolute rules to collecting.

When it comes to bicycles, older is generally more valuable than newer, but what suits you is really the best. If you restore many bikes, you'll pay more attention to the economic factor, so you can buy and sell to support your habit. Even though a 1930 Schwinn in comparable condition to a 1960 Schwinn will certainly have

The newest collectibles (latest models *and* most recent interest) are muscle bikes. Made by many manufacturers throughout the 1960s and 1970s, desirable models like this circa-1970 Schwinn Sting-Ray are not that hard to find.

A very rare model like this early 1950s Western Flyer is certainly worthy of a complete restoration. The time and expense needed to bring it back to new condition will be retained in its value.

more value, there is more to consider. First, the older bikes will, on the average, be found in lesser condition than the newer ones. This means that the restoration project will be greater in cost and time for the older bike, mainly because the real old ones usually need paint and plating. The newer old bike will certainly be easier to find, and often be in better shape than an older one when you find it. Again, the next chapter describes what is available from the various past decades.

Besides make, model, and age, color is another factor in collectibility. In the 1960s, for example, most boys' bikes were produced in red and most girls' bikes were painted blue.

From a rarity standpoint, then, a green, gold, black, or brown example is more of a standout. An original finish, regardless of color, which can be preserved, is a definite plus. Repainting is always an option, but it must be done right to maximize value, and candy colors (gold or silver undercoat with transparent color coat) are extremely difficult to apply.

Any desirable, complete (all or most of its parts intact) bicycle from the 1930s through the 1970s that you find has collectible potential. The main factor in deciding to take on the task of restoration is the bike's current condition. There is only so much time and money prudent to

spend bringing a bike back to life. A very rare, valuable bike warrants more time and money for restoration because of its potential value. The easiest place to see what kind of dollars various models in various conditions will bring is through the Internet locations described earlier, and listed in chapter 10.

There are certain conditions to avoid altogether, or conditions that relegate certain bikes to be usable for parts only. One of these conditions is any bulging in the frame or fork tubes. This problem indicates excessive rust within the tubing that has advanced beyond repair. Another bad sign is frozen bearings. Try to rotate all the bearings (fork,

Even if parts are available, it doesn't mean they are cheap. It took a few hundred dollars to buy this used chain guard for a 1937 Dayton Super Streamline.

crank, and both wheels) during your inspection. Old bicycle bearings are usually dry, or have hardened grease, but if they are totally frozen, rust is indicated. Bearings and races can be replaced, but completely seized ones may require you to replace the crank and hubs, and make fork removal impossible. If you are going to take a chance with seized bearings, make sure you buy the bike at a low price. Finally, too many missing parts make restoring some bikes prohibitive. Newer collectibles, like middleweights and Sting-Rays, have good parts availability, but that doesn't mean the parts come cheap. Older parts (pre–World War II) can add up even more, where an original seat and chain guard may cost a few hundred dollars. Check on parts availability

and price before buying a bicycle with a lot of missing pieces.

A bicycle is generally made up of painted, plated, and rubber parts. In your evaluation, you must determine if painted pieces (frame, fenders, rims, chain guard, and accessories) will require repainting, or can be preserved through cleaning, polishing, and touchup. Similarly, you must decide if plated pieces (handlebars, sprocket, rims, and fenders) will need rechroming, replacement, or can be polished and reused. Polishing at a metal plating shop can also restore alloy pieces. Additionally, decide if you've got usable pedals, seat, tires, handgrips, reflectors, and other accessory items; if not, allow room in your budget to acquire all of these needed parts.

Condition classifications run from excellent original at the top to "basket case" or parts bike at the bottom. In between are bikes of all other conditions that have the potential for improvement through restoration. These bikes are further categorized as high, average, or marginal desirability, based on what age and model they are. Strive to acquire and work with the most desirable bike in the best condition that you can, considering your abilities and resources.

One collecting guideline is universal: collect and restore what you like. The satisfaction derived from your project, and the enjoyment of ownership upon completion, will be the greatest if you really like the bike.

CHAPTER 2

Choosing the Right Project

The supply of collector bicycles spans a big condition range, while it also covers a huge spectrum of years, manufacturers, and models. Your collector bicycle search will uncover bikes ranging from complete originals to those only useful as parts donors. There are an estimated 2,000 manufacturers that operated throughout the 1900s, each making many models, so you will find a variety of choices available to you as you get into the bicycle collecting hobby.

Antiques

Antique bicycles are those from the nineteenth and early twentieth centuries. Upon the invention of the so-called "safety" bicycle—when bikes went to same-size wheels and chain drive—most early models actually began to look quite similar to their later counterparts. As previously noted, true antique bicycles have great interest and value, but the supply is too low and the cost too high to fuel the collector hobby. In the early 1900s, the "modern" design was established, but prior to 1933 almost all bikes used "single tube" tires, in which the tube was sewn into the body of the tire and then glued to the rim. These so-called "sew-up" tires are now generally used on only the most expensive racing bicycles. Handmade from silk or hi-tech materials, these tires are expensive and are still a complete pain to work with.

For the rest of us, the invention of the "wired" or "clincher" tire should be viewed as a welcome development.

Heavyweights

In 1933 the "balloon tire" era began, when Schwinn introduced its 26x2.125-inch tube-in-tire design.

The "single tube" tires used on the old bikes were of an integral tire and tube design. The single tube tires were glued to the rims, like these from a 1910 Iver Johnson. Again, these rare, costly items are not in the collecting mainstream. Note the high-wheel "boneshaker" in the background.

This quickly became the industry standard, and a period of "heavy" bicycle design ensued and continued until about 1955. Weight saving did not seem to be a concern, as "extras" were a big part of what gave these bikes the designation of "heavyweights." The most prized models of this era are the ones with lights, horns, key locks, tanks, cross-brace handlebars, and spring-type forks.

Contrary to popular belief, bicycle suspension is not a new idea. Virtually every manufacturer from this early period offered a spring-type fork or "springer" front end. The designs for this type of suspension vary greatly, as each company seemed to have a "better" way to make it. With the interchangeability among makers, it is common to find a spring-type fork made by one factory installed on a bike of a different brand. It may take a bit of research to determine if the springer on your bike actually belongs there.

Key-lock front forks also evolved during this era. Schwinn introduced the "Cyclelock" in 1935, which could be had in conjunction with the spring-front suspension. It may have added some security, but mainly added more weight and future collectibility.

The most popular heavyweights of the 1950s were the loaded models like this 1954 J.C. Higgins Deluxe. It sports balloon tires, light, tank, horn, and a unique "beehive" spring fork.

Schwinn introduced the Cyclelock in 1935 as a security feature. It actually just added some extra weight and future collectibility. This key and lock assembly is shown here on a 1950 Red Phantom.

Tanks appear on many models as a decorative touch. Here, this 1953 Schwinn Panther has an original tank designed for its straight lower frame bar. Also visible is Schwinn's patented version of a spring fork.

Fender ornaments don't get much more elaborate than this. A cast metal airplane, with a whirling propeller, was used on a 1928 Lindy bicycle.

During the heavyweight period, everything from automobiles to motorcycles to airplanes influenced manufacturers' designs. These bikes don't need fuel, but that did not stop companies from placing large tanks on their deluxe models. These tanks usually house a horn and a light and even offered space for a young rider to store his most precious treasures. Whatever their use, these tanks go a long way to giving heavyweights their distinctive look. In 1934, Arnold, Schwinn & Co. marketed a model named the Streamline Aerocycle, with a large airplane decal on the tank. The Shelby Cycle Company offered a 1928 model called a Lindy, which sported a small aeroplane fender ornament with a whirling propeller. A 1935 vintage Schwinn named Motorbike didn't even have a motor. Two other Schwinn models carried the names of Auto-Cycle, and Cycleplane, evidently connecting the image of their bicycles to cars and airplanes. Many of these Schwinn models up to about 1950 carried an Excelsior-Schwinn head badge. Schwinn had acquired the Excelsior and Henderson motorcycle companies in the early 1900s, and was still promoting these names. A natural result of this pairing was the adaptation of some motorcycle features, such as the expander brake, to bicycles.

Schwinn was a major player in the heavyweight era, especially with

line) for those on a smaller budget or with different taste.

Schwinn provided much leadership and innovation throughout the balloon tire era, but it was definitely not alone in the marketplace. The Cleveland Welding Company probably made more bicycle frames than anyone during these years. It supplied frames for a variety of independently distributed brands. This Ohio-based company supplied frames for Hiawatha, Roadmaster, Rollfast, Zenith, Elgin, Western Flyer, and Hawthorne. The Western Flyer brand was sold through Western Auto stores. The other makes were offered in a variety of outlets, except the Hawthorne, which was a Montgomery Ward exclusive.

Sears has had bicycles in its catalog since the company began in 1896. They offered a number of brands for sale, including the Elgin, which was renamed to J.C. Higgins after World War II. Sears sold the J.C. Higgins brand through the 1950s, and after that time, their bikes began to carry a Sears nameplate. Because of Sears' market penetration and good reputation, these bikes were sold in huge numbers. This translates to a good supply in today's collector market. The J.C. Higgins bicycle, like other makes, came in standard and deluxe versions. A deluxe model had it all: balloon tires, tank, lights, horn, racks, reflectors, rear-wheel skirt guards, finned coaster brake hub, spring-type fork, and more. Like their counterparts in other makes, the early J.C. Higgins models more than lived up to their heavyweight designation by tipping the scales at 60–65 pounds.

All of the brands had an example of a "more is better" model, exemplifying an exercise in excess. Today these models are among the most sought

The early Schwinn models (up to about 1950) used Excelsior badges, as Schwinn owned the Excelsior and Henderson motorcycle companies. Evidently, they wanted to associate their bicycles with motorcycles.

its Phantom series. The Black Phantom, introduced in 1949, was and remains the most popular, but all Phantoms were not black. A Green Phantom and a Red Phantom were offered during the 1950s as well, and to the collector, these versions may prove to be the biggest of finds from that era. Many kids wanted these loaded models, but not all parents could afford them. There were also many standard, simpler models (like Hornet and Spitfire in the Schwinn

The deluxe J.C. Higgins models (like other brands) came with a lot of goodies, such as the skirt guards on the rear wheel of this 1948.

Special touches, like the finned rear hub (for style *and* improved brake cooling), appeared on deluxe models. This spotless example is attached to the rear wheel of a 1954 J.C. Higgins.

The cast metal headlight alone on this early 1950s Western Flyer X53 is responsible for a good portion of the bike's total weight. Like automobiles of the era, saving weight just was not a design consideration.

after. Western Flyer, for example, made an X53 Special for two years only. This model was not into weight saving, as made evident by its stout, cast metal headlight, along with the other typical goodies of the period.

You will discover many other makes from this heavyweight period, including Monark, Evans, Colson, Dayton, Belknap, Murray, and Columbia. Even the tire companies wanted bikes with their names attached, so Goodyear, Firestone, and B.F. Goodrich contracted with various manufacturers to supply special models bearing those labels. You will see the names of many different makers on the rear hub coaster brake arms also. Common brands of hubs you'll encounter are Bendix, Peerless, New Departure, and Morrow. If it reads "J.C. Higgins" or "Schwinn Approved," it's hard to tell who made it, as both companies subcontracted most of their "private label" stock parts.

Precise dating is difficult for most of the brands, with the exception of Columbia and Schwinn models. These two makes used a systematic, chronological serial numbering system, which designates the month and year of manufacture. For example, a Schwinn serial number is stamped under the crank bottom bracket before about 1953, on the left rear dropout circa 1953 through 1969, and on the head tube after that. Generally, the first number in the sequence designates the year on early models (pre-1965), and the second letter is a code for the year on later models. A Schwinn with serial number J164477 stamped on the left rear dropout is a 1961 model. A Schwinn with serial number DB41034 on the dropout is a 1966 model, because the second-letter code starts with a 1965 model being "A." This letter code continues

Bendix supplied many hubs for Schwinn and other brands. They even came out with an automatic two-speed in the 1960s. Gears are changed by rotating the pedals backward slightly on this "kick-back" hub, eliminating the need for a cable.

through the next 20 years, except "I" and "O" are not used.

Most Schwinn dealers can give you this information if you supply them with a serial number from your Schwinn. Both the Schwinn and Columbia listings can also be found in bicycle history books (Schwinn-Built Bicycles by James Hurd & T.A. Gordon, for example), and at some of the bicycle websites on the Internet. Generally though, if an old bicycle has a 2-1/8-inch tire width, it's between a 1933 and 1955 model. You can also bet it is not a 1942, 1943, 1944, or 1945 vintage. As with

automobiles, civilian bicycle models were not offered during the war, and stripped-down, no-frills, no-chrome military models are next to impossible to find. Columbia offered a limited number of folding military-style bikes called the Victory to the public, but they're scarce enough that finding one now is unlikely.

The aesthetic allure of the heavyweight models is indisputable, but sadly, they are difficult to find in decent condition because of their age. Simply due to the time that they have been around (50 years or more), they are more likely to have rust, dry bearings,

The advent of the middleweights (1954) brought a narrower tire (1-3/4 inch) and lighter components. They were still heavy bikes, but were designed to compete with the lighter imports and still be durable.

A late 1950s Schwinn Jaguar is a fairly heavy middleweight, but manufacturers were experimenting to compete with the imports. This model even has a British Sturmey-Archer three-speed cable-controlled hub.

missing or non-original parts, plus a need for painting and plating. This does not diminish the appeal of these nifty relics, but generally means greater cost and time will be spent on the restoration of a heavyweight. For example, a heavyweight's leather seat has a lot of character, but it's hard to find a usable one, and using a restoration service for one of these seats is expensive. Reproduction leather seats are available but also not cheap. Just remember to be realistic in planning your project; if it is your first restoration, don't take on too much.

Middleweights

After World War II, the bicycle market took right off again. The enlarged market of the baby boomer population was soon to come, for which there would be a new product offering. This new bicycle came to market as a middleweight design—sort of a cross between the old heavyweight and the imported lightweights that were gaining some market share. Middleweight sales points were that they rode easier than the heavyweights but were more durable than the lightweight imports. It should be noted that Schwinn had always made

lightweights also, but they were only promoted to the smaller markets of adults and competitive riders. With the imports starting to market to this huge new youth population, American manufacturers responded with the middleweight models. To compete with the lightweight competition, some middleweight models were even offered with two- and three-speed rear hubs.

As typical, Schwinn took the lead with its introduction of the middleweight Corvette model in 1954. The new model had a slightly lighter frame, fewer add-on accessories, and a new 1-3/4-inch rim width. Schwinn patented this rim design, and that's why other middleweight manufacturers used a rim designation of 1.75, which uses a tire with a different bead type. The new Schwinn design was called an S-7 straight-side tubular rim, replacing the wider, heavier S-2. Although these bikes were still relatively heavy, the changes were effective in reducing weight and increasing ease of riding.

The middleweights were a market success. By 1956 virtually every American bicycle manufacturer's line was dominated with this new style. Because of the bicycles' continued popularity, combined with the huge "boomer" market, millions of middleweights were sold from 1955 to 1969, and even later in lesser numbers.

In today's marketplace, the supply of vintage middleweights is plentiful. You will, of course, uncover many manufacturers representing this period as you scour the market. Sears continued its success in selling bicycles, but somewhere around 1960, dropped the J.C. Higgins designation and simply called their bikes "Sears." Sears, like others, didn't give up on the aero association when they shifted to middleweight design. In fact, two of their models were the Flightliner and the Spaceliner. They did not abandon accessories totally either, as lights, horns, and tanks still appeared on these models, but with an increased reliance on plastic. Do you like chrome? Great, then look for one of the early 1960s all-chrome models from Sears. Besides the typical chrome parts, even the frame is chrome, and the bike features many chromed plastic parts, such as a decorative sprocket cover.

Two other catalog stores continued to sell bicycles through the 1950s and 1960s: Montgomery Ward and J.C. Penney. The Hawthorne models from Wards sold better than the

Kids were making their own muscle bikes even before the factories did. This 1961, 20-inch Schwinn Tornado became a homemade Sting-Ray with the addition of a banana seat and high rise handlebars.

Penney's model called Foremost. This is evident, as today's market availability of vintage Hawthornes far exceeds the supply of Foremosts. Both models were available in boys', girls', loaded, and basic versions.

Other makes that were manufactured and marketed as middleweights in this period are: Columbia, Western Flyer, Murray, Huffy, Evans, and Roadmaster (AMF). Youth is an advantage when it comes to bicycles. The "younger" middleweights (compared to heavyweights) are available in greater numbers, and have improved odds of being in better condition. Your chance of finding a mostly complete, collectible middleweight with acceptable paint is very good. This type of old original bike will still be challenging and fun to restore. It's best to get familiar with bikes through an "easier" (not needing paint or a lot of parts) restoration, before taking on a major project.

The disc brake option on this 1971 Schwinn Sting-Ray Orange Krate is rare and desirable in today's collector's market.

The Krate series employed a stick shift to change gears on the derailleur models.

Based on collectors' past habits, you will probably restore and collect more than one bike.

Middleweight model lineups began having more of the multisized bicycle offerings than before. While most bicycles in both heavyweight and middleweight designs were sold in the 26-inch version, the middleweight 20-inch and 24-inch models were available in greater numbers during the late 1950s and throughout the 1960s than previously. Still, the 26-inch version sold well and was the bike for the younger owner of a 20- or 24-inch bicycle to move up to. This way, a manufacturer could develop brand loyalty by getting a customer to start with their smaller product and grow into the larger models. This move upward in size was going to change, though, as the muscle bikes were about to go to market.

Muscle Bikes

The muscle-bike movement had subtle beginnings, but quickly turned into a true market phenomenon in about 1963. In keeping with the car-customizing trend with its roots there, kids in California began customizing 20-inch bikes with "high rise" handlebars and "banana" seats. In virtually no time, manufacturers began making factory "customs," most notably the 1963 Sting-Ray introduced by Schwinn. This model and its many variations were terrific sellers to kids of all ages throughout the next 10 years and beyond. Schwinn Sting-Rays didn't own the total market, as similar bikes from other makers were offered, such as Sears Screamer, Murray Eliminator, Huffy Slingshot, and Raleigh Chopper. Schwinn was dominant in this market segment, though, especially with the success of their "Krate" series.

The white Sting-Ray Cotton Picker was the least popular of the Krate series when new. That probably makes this 1970 model even more collectible today.

Beginning in 1963 with the basic Sting-Ray, Schwinn's line of muscle bikes grew quickly. They soon added models such as the Super Deluxe, Mini-Twinn (tandem), and the legendary Krates. The original popularity of these models has carried over to the present, and they make up a big part of today's bicycle-collecting hobby, causing a lot of parts gathering and restoration activity. The Schwinn Super Deluxe Sting-Ray came factory equipped with a spring-type front fork fashioned from their 1930s design—an interesting blend of new and old. Optional equipment like disc brakes, and exclusive accessories (speedometer, turn signals, etc.), also added to the mystique. Other Sting-Ray variations like the Twinn, the Runabout (quick-release

fold-down), and the 24-inch Manta Ray didn't sell that well but created future collectibles.

The Krate series, sold by Schwinn from 1968 to 1973, set the standard for the "muscle"- or "chopper"-type bicycle. In the early 1970s you could choose from an Orange Krate, Apple Krate, Lemon Peeler, Pea Picker, Grey Ghost, or a Cotton Picker. This list of models, according to Kathy Bruce, a Schwinn dealer, is in order of original sales popularity, with the Orange Krate selling best. These interesting Sting-Rays were further factory "modified" with a smaller 16-inch front rim, spring fork, derailleur rear hub (some with stick shift), and more, to add to their exciting appeal. These chopper-style Krates, like some bikes of the 1930s,

Whizzers open up a whole new area of collecting and restoring. The engine and extra mechanical components require additional expertise to repair and restore.

emulated motorcycle designs. There is something about the Krate bikes that makes it easy to imagine you have an engine aboard. The Krates, along with the standard Sting-Rays and other brand muscle bikes, brought plenty of interest to the bicycle hobby, which continues fervently with the collectors of today.

Muscle bikes, especially Sting-Rays, are great collectible bikes for several reasons. Their relatively young age means that they will generally be found in better condition than bikes twice as old. These bicycles sold in such great numbers, that large quantities are still around today. The current popularity of the Sting-Ray models is so high that aftermarket suppliers now sell reproduction parts, such as fenders and seats. These and other factors place Sting-Rays, led by the Krate series, among the most-sought-after collector bicycles in history.

Other Models of Interest

The tendency of bicycle manufacturers to emulate motorcycles, automobiles, and airplanes has been discussed. One of the most obvious examples of this is the motorized Whizzer. The early 1940s seemed like the right time to motorize a bicycle. The Whizzer Company developed a four-stroke engine designed to be adapted to heavyweight bicycles. It caught the attention of Schwinn's management, always on top of innovation, and a mutual deal was struck. By the latter 1940s, most of the Whizzer motorbikes were sold with Schwinn frames. The earliest (circa 1939) Whizzer Model D used an inefficient friction drive. The later models E, F, H (postwar, with 200,000 unit sales), and J used a belt drive system that worked better. Restoring a Whizzer requires much research and mechanical ability; they are also a

fairly pricey commodity. The scarcity of the Whizzer, combined with its popularity, has caused the motorbike's recent rerelease under the same Whizzer name. The brand-new ones are likely to be instantly collectible.

Lightweight models must be mentioned in any collectible bicycle discussion. The old ones are collectible for sure; it's just harder to find them, because fewer were sold.

Lightweights were manufactured by American corporations (again, notably Arnold, Schwinn & Co.) right along with the heavyweights, middleweights, and muscle bikes. The lightweights just never had the same emotional appeal as their nifty, heavier counterparts. Alas, these lighter models were for practical riding, not what most kids are looking for. American lightweights were also market victim to less expensive import models. Remember: England

and other European countries were making bikes all along too; in fact, American manufacturers used many import parts, such as pedals from the German-based Union Company. Predictably, the American models were still heavier than their import competition. One reason for that is because many of the American lightweights share parts with the heavyweight models. If you come across an excellent lightweight, you will probably want it. There are many desirable American and imported lightweights that are worth collecting. Even a not-so-rare newer lightweight in poor condition may have valuable parts that will fit on other bicycle types.

Tandems certainly are not near the top of the list for collectibility. Maybe it's like car collecting: two-door cars are generally preferred to otherwise equivalent four-door cars. The concept of two seats on a bicycle is apparently too practical or something. Actually, once you've ridden an old tandem, they seem more like an amusement park ride than something practical. "Two seaters" (also some three, four, and more seaters) have been built throughout the entire twentieth century, and whether heavy, middle, or light versions, they all weigh a lot. You will notice very heavy gauge spokes on these models, along with larger frame tubing, bigger hubs, and other heavier duty parts than the single-rider bikes. As with lightweights and true antique bicycles, there can't be a large collector market, because fewer of these bikes were manufactured to begin with. There is some interest in all bicycle models, and there are specialized collectors who seek only tandems, Whizzers, classic racing bikes, or even the most obscure model.

There are still other special interest bicycles, but most of them fall into that low supply or high dollar category (or both). An example is the limited production Bowden Spacelander of the late 1950s, which makes a bold design statement with its streamlined fiberglass molded frame. There were only about 500 of these made to begin with, and less than 100 are still around today.

The bicycle collecting and restoring hobby can go in many directions, from general to very specific interest. Many different tastes exist, and only you know what you like.

If you're not sure what you like, have fun exploring all the possibilities!

Very early Whizzers (late 1930s) used a friction drive on the rear tire. That design was quickly abandoned in favor of this belt-drive system.

CHAPTER 3

Planning the Restoration

L et's think about the "re" words: restore, recondition, redo, renew, repair, refresh, refurbish, renovate, re-plate, and repaint. Then consider two more: reuse and replace. All the parts of your bicycle will fall into either the "reuse" or "replace" category. For the parts in the "replace" category, you might find NOS (New old stock, unused vintage parts) or reproductions that are ready to install. For all other parts (reused or replacement used), you will have to perform one of the tasks implied by the preceding "re" word list. Definitions vary, but all the words suggest an attempt to make something like new again. This is what you will strive for in your project. The adage, "A whole is the sum of its parts," is truly appropriate in bicycle restoration. When you concentrate on making each and every part the very best it can be, you will assemble a whole bike that will make you proud.

The last word on that "re" list— repaint—brings up a very important consideration in restoration: to paint or not to paint? It really is an important question, which was touched upon in the introduction of this book but warrants further mention. In a fairly recent trend, original finishes on any collectibles have been gaining favor. An excellent original finish on a piece of furniture, a car, toy, or bicycle will out-value an otherwise equivalent example that has been refinished. It is for that reason (and

Certain parts, like this circa-1930 leather seat replica, are available as reproductions. Also notice the replica pant leg clamps, which were used when riding early models without chain guards.

Don't rule out a full repaint and restoration for a rare bike like this 1930s Belknap. Just be prepared to spend the time and money to do it right.

You've chosen your bike, have a plan of attack, and are ready to dive in—almost. A shortage of proper tools and supplies to support your plan of action is frustrating. Interrupting your work time with shopping trips for tools and supplies gets tiresome. In addition to having a well-lit, clean workplace of ample size, there are some standard and specialized tools you'll need, as well as some other products. The use of these tools and products will be explained in subsequent chapters. What follows is a general description of these items to help you prepare for work on an old bike.

First, if you have or can borrow a bicycle stand, you will appreciate it. Unless you have many bicycles, however, it is probably the least-needed tool for use in your restoration. Most hobbyists get by just fine without

the time and cost of refinishing) that finding a bike with original paint that can be preserved with cleaning and touchup should be your goal. Even with its imperfections, and possibly even because of its flaws (a built-in history), the bike will be desirable and look great. Remember: there are lots of parts on a bike to work on besides the paint. Painting should not be ruled out for full restoration of a very rare bike (one that will have a high value when complete) that is currently a basket case, or in the building of a custom bicycle designed to your own taste. Chapter 7 describes the work involved in the painting process. As a reminder, don't get involved in a painting project if you are not willing to devote the time to do it right. It can't be stressed too much that when it comes to paint, either you will work very hard or pay a professional very well to achieve excellent results. Shortcuts do not produce excellent results, and original paint, regardless of condition, is better than a poor repaint.

Before starting your restoration, identify and list missing or broken parts needing replacement. This is an ongoing process, beginning with the selection of your project bike. You shouldn't have chosen a bike with lots of missing parts to begin with, but you'll surely discover worn or incorrect parts needing replacement as you do your work.

Depending on the make and model, your parts can be easy or difficult to locate. Bearings, for example, are readily available at bike shops. Decals, accessories, and certain mechanical parts are found at specialty suppliers (catalog/mail order). Things such as seats, chain guards, or spring forks for old, rare models require some searching. Chapter 10 lists some of these parts sources. It is best to know what parts you need, and if you can get them, before getting started. There's no reason to begin a stock restoration of a rare model with missing fenders, seat, chain guard, and rear hub if there are no parts available for it.

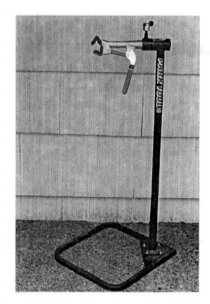

If you have, or can borrow, a bike stand like this one, you will appreciate it. It is not a necessary tool for your restoration, however, and most hobbyists get by without one. Consider one if you're servicing and maintaining several bikes.

Most hobbyists interviewed just place their bicycles upside down as shown on a sheet, or other protective surface, for disassembly.

Your bike may or may not have a master link on its chain. Chains without a master link require a chain rivet extractor to take them apart. This tool is also needed for any chain when adding or subtracting links. Never, never try the hammer and nail method for this procedure; the proper tool is readily available at bike shops and is not very expensive. The chain rivet tool, often called a Rivoli, is designed to push chain rivets out and back in without damage to the chain or rivets.

one. One of the purposes of a bicycle stand is to get the bike to a height where you don't have to bend over or be on your knees to work on it. Of course once a bike is disassembled, the parts can be placed on a workbench. If you have a good vise, a bike can be placed in it by flattening an old seat post on one end and using it to affix the bike to the vise; just place the flattened seat post firmly in the vise, and slide the bike frame onto the round end of the seat post, in its original location in the frame. Again, most hobbyists interviewed just place the bike upside down on a sheet or tarp for disassembly, assembly, maintenance, and adjustments.

A spoke wrench is a tool well worth obtaining. With the tire removed, you can tighten spokes with a screwdriver, but the majority of spoke adjustment is done with a spoke wrench. On some bikes, you will see gouges and other marks on the spoke nipples, which are from the use of improper tools, like pliers. Spoke

wrenches are made in individual sizes or a more universal, multisized version. These wrenches are designed to fit the flat spots on the spoke nipples securely, and rotate them easily and without damage. Spoke wrenches are available at all bicycle shops.

Another tool available at all bicycle shops is a set of tire irons. You can get a tire off its rim by other means, like using screwdrivers, but they can scratch your rim, ruin an inner tube, and cut your tire. After all, tire irons are inexpensive and work well. They are designed to minimize the chance of damaging the tire bead and tube. The tire irons usually come in a set of three, which is kind of like having an extra hand when it comes to tire removal. Crank Brothers makes a nifty little tool that allows you to quickly remove a tire and then re-seat the bead when you replace it. It's a nice, inexpensive tool that works much like the tire machine at your local auto mechanic's, except that it's plastic and fits in your pocket.

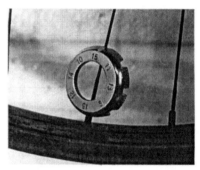

A good spoke wrench is a must for spoke adjustment. They are available in individual sizes or universal fit models, such as the one shown here. These are purchased from bicycle shops, and allow you to turn the spoke nipples without damaging them.

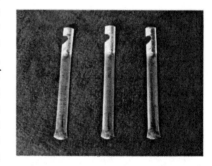

You can buy a set of bicycle tire irons at any bicycle shop. They are considerably easier to use than screwdrivers and are designed to lessen the occurrence of tube damage and avoid damage to your painted or chromed rim.

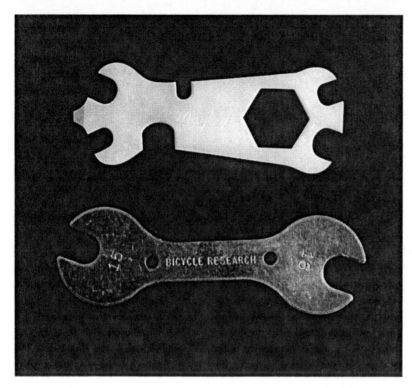

A professional truing stand, like the one in this bike shop, is available for purchase by a consumer. Unless you're truing a lot of wheels, it might be best to let the bike mechanic do it for you.

Hub wrenches come in a variety of shapes and sizes. Their main feature is their thinness, which allows them to fit the narrow slots on hub-bearing cones.

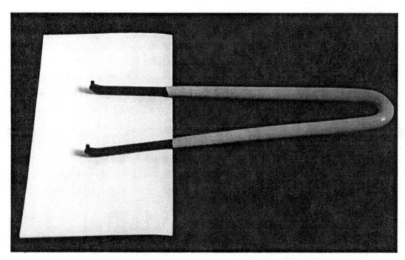

This flat-blade spanner wrench fits the two slots in the crank-bearing cone on most early bikes with one-piece cranks. You can purchase one at any bicycle shop.

If you wish to experiment with wheel truing, a home version of a truing stand can be fashioned as shown. Spring clamps are used as reference points to detect wobble.

Small things are easy to overlook. Make sure you have some sort of valve stem core-removal tool on hand. The one shown in the picture is handy, because it can extract a broken core and clean up the stem threads.

Hub wrenches are necessary to fit hub-bearing cones. There is a locknut that holds the bearing cones in position, and the clearance between the nut and the hub is so small, a thin wrench is needed to hold the bearing cone. These thin hub wrenches—or "cone" wrenches—are sold at bike shops in metric and standard sizes. Many hubs even on very old bikes use metric sizes, because of their European origin. In an emergency, you can grind down a cheap wrench on a grinding wheel to make the wrench thinner and to fit the narrow gap.

The adjustable bearing race on the crank is easier to turn and adjust by using a wrench called a spanner. For one-piece cranks, a flat-blade version is correct. Some rear hubs, especially multi-sprocket clusters, also use a spanner nut. Any bearing cone or

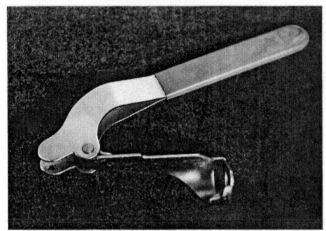

This specialty tool is for removing and installing Schwinn built-in kickstands. It makes the job a snap, but there is another way to service these kickstands shown in chapter 4.

nut with two slots or holes used for turning it is turned best with a spanner wrench. You can use a screwdriver for this purpose if necessary, but if much pressure is required, great care must be taken not to damage the holes or slots. To avoid damaging parts, it's best to buy and use a spanner wrench.

When you get around to removing the bearing cups in the bottom bracket and the fork tube, make certain that you have a sturdy dowel (like part of a broom handle), a brass drift (cylindrical brass bar), or an old aluminum seat post as a pounding aid. Something about 8 or 9 inches in length is ideal for this purpose.

A wheel-truing stand is another of the items that you should consider only if you'll work on many bikes. Most of us have the aptitude to true a bicycle wheel but only with much practice. Getting the feel of spoke tension, and its effect on a rim, is definitely a learned ability. You can experiment with any rim by using an old front fork, placed upside down in a vise or fabricated stand. A commercial truing stand has built-in brackets and calipers to reference the trueness of a wheel; your home-built version can employ clamps of some type to duplicate this feature (see photo). Also, use a felt-tip marker or chalk for marking a rim while truing it. After reading chapter 5 and experimenting with truing, you should not feel bad about referring this task to your local bike mechanic, if it seems too tough.

A vise is handy in any shop, so of course your bicycle shop could use

Portable compressed air is an alternative to a costly compressor. Tanks like this are not too expensive and after being filled, let you have air when and where you need it.

one. Some hobbyists like to use them for pressing in bearing cups, but it isn't a necessity. If you have a vise, you'll use it for sure, but if you don't have a vise, don't buy one just for bicycle work.

Now we're down to the more standard tools: hammers, wrenches, pliers, and screwdrivers. For hammers, hard- and soft-faced types are nice to have. Depending on the size, the hard-faced hammer can deliver a sharper blow than the soft-faced model. The urethane-coated or rubber hammers can strike parts like bearing cups directly, without damage to the parts. If the hard-faced hammer is used on any visible parts, protect the parts from the hammer with a block of wood.

Have wrenches of the combination (open end/box end) variety available, along with a good adjustable wrench. Locking pliers

(like Vise-Grip), groove-joint pliers (like Channelock), and regular pliers will be used. Screwdrivers (usually flat blade) in long, short, and even "L" shape are useful.

Compressed air is used for much more than filling tire tubes. You will appreciate having an air nozzle for aid in cleaning and drying parts, and even for handgrip removal (see chapter 4). If you don't have an air compressor, you should at least get a tank designed for holding compressed air. These are filled from a compressor and give you portable compressed air wherever you need it. If you plan on painting with a paint gun, however, you will need a compressor.

Goggles (eye protection) and rubber gloves are a must when working with certain tools and chemicals. Follow all manufacturers' recommendations for use. For painting, it is highly recommended that you use a

respirator approved for the purpose (shown in chapter 7), along with a designated painting area.

Steel wool has long been a favorite tool of auto and bicycle restorers and detailers. An auto detail shop is one place to find the proper "00" or "000" (double ought or triple ought) steel wool, which will not scratch the plated surfaces. It is not to be used on paint, except for the possible removal of old paint, when trying to uncover an original finish. Rust removal from plated surfaces is where this tool "shines." This type of polishing steel wool is also available at hardware stores and auto paint suppliers.

Various brushes are good for cleaning dirt, grease, and even rust. For rust removal, brass brushes do the most good with the least harm. You will use other brushes in conjunction with cleaners and degreasers to get parts clean.

Throughout your project, you will want penetrating oil, spray lube/solvent (like WD-40), bearing lubricant (in bulk, and a squeeze tube for "injecting" bearings), chain lubricant, degreaser (solvent or thinner), and a spray cleaner (Brakleen or Lectra-Motive) by your side. As usual, follow manufacturers' warnings and recommendations when using the caustic products.

Finally, to help control the messes you make, have plenty of towels at your disposal. Standard paper towels, blue paper shop towels, old terry cloth towels, and old T-shirts will all serve a purpose in the work you are about to do.

Some tools to go along with your compressed air are an air blower nozzle, air delivery chuck, and a reliable pressure gauge. At lower right is a special multipurpose tool for removing the valve core from an inner tube.

CHAPTER 4

Disassembly

Required Tools

Wrenches, combination
and adjustable
Pliers, locking and
groove-joint
Screwdrivers, standard and
Phillips, long and short
Hammer and wood block
Large dowel or old seat post
Valve stem tool
Penetrating oil
Goggles
Rags

Recommended Tools

Bicycle tire irons
Spanner wrench
Brass drift
Soft-faced hammer
Compressed air
Chain rivet tool
Kickstand tool
Vise
Bicycle stand
Sheet or tarp
Sandwich bags for
small parts

Any bicycle restoration must begin with disassembly. From a basic cleaning and lubrication to a major restoration, taking the bike apart is the first step. This allows you to get a close look at parts and pieces for further evaluation. Now is the time to gather your tools and supplies, put the bike in your chosen workplace, and get busy!

The bicycle featured for disassembly is a 1960s vintage, and was chosen for its completeness and originality. As recognized and discussed in other chapters, some bikes will have missing or incorrect parts, and condition will vary greatly. The procedures henceforth apply to bicycles made throughout the 1900s, and certain exceptions for different models and conditions will be noted. Always follow the manufacturer's safety recommendations when using tools and chemicals. If in doubt, err on the side of caution, especially with caustic chemicals, solvents, and paints.

Begin by spraying penetrating oil or parts loosener on every visible bolt, screw, and nut. Avoid overspray on painted graphics and decals as much as possible.

Take pictures of the bike and its assemblies before they come apart. Throughout disassembly, take shots of as many areas as possible. It may be awhile before you reassemble the bike, and a photo reference is helpful at that time. Photos will also be an aid to you in research and in conversations with hobbyists and professionals.

Remove accessories such as baskets, front or rear carriers, bags, horns, lights, or tanks at any time appropriate, along with the following operations.

Handgrips

Like all projects, there must be a starting point. Remove the handgrips in almost every case. The exception would be if an original set of good grips has been glued to a good set of handlebars that will not be plated or replaced.

Removing the grips should be easy, if someone has not glued them (no glue or adhesive should be used on handgrips). Sometimes, just twisting the grip with your hand will loosen it and allow the grip to be pulled off. A great method (if not glued) is to use compressed air. Hopefully, you have an air canister, or compressor, previously recommended. Shoot air into the hole in one grip, while tightly covering the hole of the other grip. The grip that is the loosest will come off first. After one is off, hold your palm over the hole in the

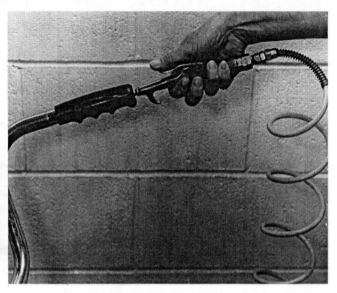

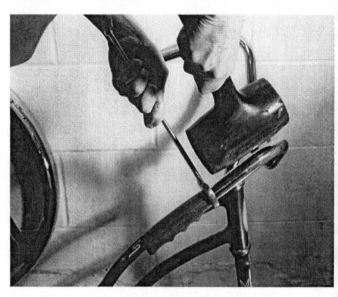

Compressed air is the best "tool" for handgrip removal. Here, a cushion of air is forced between the grip and the handlebar, helping the grip slide off.

A sharp blow to an open-end wrench (usually 7/8 inch), placed against the grip, is another way to dislodge a stubborn grip.

bare handlebar, while shooting air in the hole of the remaining grip. Now, or maybe with the help of a little twisting, the grip should "blow" right off. The compressed air expands the grip slightly, breaking the seal of the grip to the bar.

Use a utility (razor) knife to remove handgrips that have been glued on. Again, if you can reuse the grips, if the bars do not need plating (chroming), and if the grips are glued, just leave them in place. If you are going to re-plate the bars, or if the grips are to be replaced (due to wear or incorrectness), just cut off the glued-on grips.

An alternate method makes use of a standard 7/8-inch (for most handlebars) combination wrench. Place the open end of the wrench on the bar, and slide it up next to the grip. Tap the wrench with a hammer. The impact will usually remove a grip that is not glued on.

Whether saved or not, remove the grips if the handlebars are to be removed from the stem clamp for any reason. Store the removed grips

where they will be safe from solvents or other damage.

Turn It Over

There are such things as bicycle stands, designed for holding bikes during maintenance and repair. With

a stand, you can rotate the bike 360 degrees and work at any height you wish. These are handy, but unless you are going to work on many bikes, are probably not needed for the average do-it-yourselfer. Simply placing the bike upside down on a protective

This upside-down position allows you access and provides stability for most disassembly operations. Here, the bike is shown on an old bed sheet, with tools and workbench close by.

Typical front chain guard attachment is screw and nut. Move the wrench while holding the screw for best leverage. There should be a lock washer on this application.

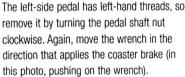

The left-side pedal has left-hand threads, so remove it by turning the pedal shaft nut clockwise. Again, move the wrench in the direction that applies the coaster brake (in this photo, pushing on the wrench).

sheet or blanket will allow you to perform most operations satisfactorily.

Pedals

Pedals vary in style, but they are all removed about the same. If your bike has working coaster brakes and the chain is attached, this operation is easier. There are common right-hand threads on the right-side (from seated, forward-facing viewpoint) pedal, and left-hand threads on the left pedal. This means that you remove the right-side pedal by turning the pedal shaft a typical counterclockwise direction (looking at the outside end of the pedal), and you rotate the reverse-threaded left-side pedal axle the less-typical clockwise direction for removal.

Now the working coaster brake advantage: just turn the pedal shafts (with wrench on the pedal "nut" next to crank) in the direction that applies the brakes. This backward motion is the proper removal direction for both left and right pedals. The action of the brake holds the crank from turning, while you apply leverage with the wrench to remove the pedals.

If the bicycle does not have a coaster brake, or if the chain is missing, you must hold the crank stationary while removing the pedals.

Chain Guard

If you are lucky enough to have a chain guard, taking it off should be easy. Most chain guards are attached with screws fore and aft. The front screw usually has a nut attached, and you can remove it with a wrench and screwdriver. Use a screwdriver that fills up the screw slot's length and width, to keep from damaging the screw. Also, turn the nut first, while holding the screw, to use maximum leverage on a tight or rusty connection.

The rear of the chain guard might be attached with a screw threaded into the frame or with a band that wraps around the frame's right chain-stay (similar to the coaster brake arm clamp usually attached to the left side). In either case, simply remove the screw, and the chain guard should come off.

In some cases, screws may snap or may have been replaced with improper (too long, too small, wrong shape) fasteners, making replacement necessary.

Use recloseable sandwich bags to separate, store, and identify all the small parts you are taking off.

Before removing the nuts completely, note arrangement of washers, braces, and brackets. Typical order is shown here.

This bike has the fender-to-fork screw on the underside of the fender; some are on top. You can remove any hex-head screw with a small socket, if it is too stubborn to break loose with a screwdriver.

Now is a good time to have some reclosable sandwich bags for storing small parts and fasteners. Identify the bag's contents with a permanent felt marker or with a slip of paper inside the bag. Keep any chain guard screws (and other small parts to come) bagged, identified, and separate from other screws, washers, nuts, and bolts.

Front-Wheel Assembly

This removal operation is not difficult, but take some extra care. Before removing the axle nuts completely, note the arrangement of nuts, washers, fender braces, and any other brackets or accessories attached at this location. This will be reference for future reassembly. As ever, take photos before disassembly to be certain how it was. Even if the assembly is incorrect, the photos are helpful for evaluation and research.

Loosen the axle nuts with the appropriate wrench (a good-fitting one to avoid nut damage), and remove them. Loosen both nuts in the typical counterclockwise direction.

Pull fender braces free from axle shaft at this time. A bicycle with a spring fork, book carrier, basket, or speedometer will have additional attachments to the front axle shaft. These items are also held by the axle nut, so remove them now. Finally, lift the wheel assembly out of the fork.

Front Fender

Fenders might be painted or chromed, and have one or two sets of braces. The braces are attached to the axle shaft and come right off after the axle nut is removed. The remaining screw holding the fender to the fork is either on the top or underside of the fender. Remove this screw, and lift the fender right out.

Loosen the crank nut with an adjustable wrench by turning the nut clockwise (in this photo, pushing down on the wrench). If the chain is on and the coaster brake works, the brake will hold the crank still during this operation.

A flat-blade spanner wrench is the best tool to use here, minimizing the chance of damage to the slots.

Note the arrangement and position of these parts for future assembly.

Crank

The common, older bicycle crank is one piece, with a left-hand threaded nut and bearing race holding it in place. As with the pedals, the removal direction for the crank nut is the direction that applies the coaster brake. When looking straight at the nut, the rotation should be clockwise to loosen the nut. This is the opposite of typical loosening, because of the left-hand thread.

After the nut and washer are removed, spin off the bearing race (also known as an adjusting cone). You can do this with a screwdriver, using the slots on the bearing race. If a screwdriver is used, be careful not to damage the slot. The preferred tool for this, especially during final assembly and adjustment, is a wrench called a flat-blade pin spanner, available at a bike shop.

With the crank nut and bearing race unthreaded, the bearing will be visible. Note the arrangement and positions of these parts, and remove them. Now remove the crank from the frame as you lift the chain off the sprocket.

If you are working on an import lightweight or a racing bike, you may encounter a three-piece crank assembly. The crank arms holding the pedals actually come off of the crank axle, so that you can remove the crank's axle shaft and the bearings from the bottom bracket. A certain old Iver-Johnson model sports a two-piece crank as another variation. With few exceptions, the bikes described and discussed here will have the traditional one-piece crank.

If plating or replacement of the sprocket is desired, you must remove the sprocket from the crank. To do this, simply unscrew the bearing cone (which has two flat sides to accommodate a large wrench) by turning it counterclockwise. This cone is attached to the crank with threads and holds the sprocket to the crank.

Loosen the rear axle nuts by turning them counterclockwise with the proper wrench.

Note the arrangement and position of all parts prior to wheel removal.

Rear-Wheel Assembly

Generally, older bicycles have coaster brakes, and the coaster brake arm must be detached from the frame in order to get the rear-wheel assembly off. A screw and nut attach the arm to the frame via a band or bracket. Simply loosen and remove this screw and nut, and pull the arm out of the band. Once you've pulled the brake arm, bag and identify the nut and screw. This is an easy way to ensure that you don't lose this important piece.

Some models may have a cable-operated three-speed hub, and loosening the threaded union near the axle nut will separate the shifting cable.

Now back off the axle nuts (both are normal right-hand thread) by turning them counterclockwise with the proper wrench.

As always, check the order and position of parts before removing the wheel. Also, models with rear carriers,

baskets, or other accessories may have attachments at the rear axle position. Remove these at this time.

Now slide the rear-wheel assembly out of the frame. Lift the chain off the rear sprocket as this is done. For now, just let the loose chain rest on the frame, protecting the paint with a rag if you wish. Chain removal will be covered soon.

Rear Fender

The painted or chromed rear fender is usually attached very securely. Typically, two sets of braces, plus two frame mounting positions, are used.

The rear fender braces are not affixed at the axle nut position, as the rear-wheel assembly must be movable for chain adjustment. Braces have their own mounting point on the frame and are commonly secured with a screw, lock washer, and nut.

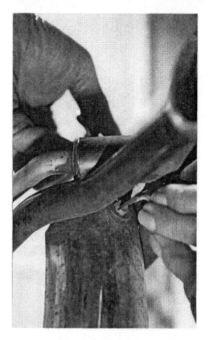

The clearance is tight at this lower front portion of the rear fender. An "L"-shaped screwdriver works well to hold the screw here.

Looking directly at the master link, place thumbs on both sides of it, and pull the chain back toward you with remaining fingers, while pressing thumbs in the opposite direction. The two pegs in the master link must be moved closer to each other so the top of the link will come off.

Once the master link cap is "popped" off and the back of the master link (with pegs) is pulled out, remove the chain.

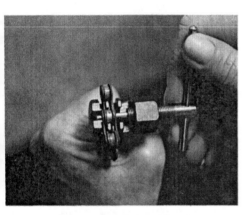

You must use a chain tool like this to remove any other chain rivets or links. Here, the tool safely pushes out a rivet.

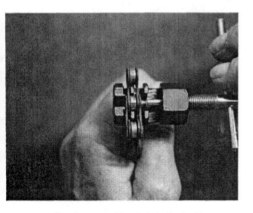

Simply reverse the chain in the tool to replace a rivet and press the rivet back into place.

Break loose the fender brace-to-frame screws by holding the screw and turning the nut with the wrench for leverage. Spin the screws out with the screwdriver to free both sets of braces.

Another rear fender connecting point is at the frame, near the seat. A short screwdriver is often needed for this tight spot. On some models, a hand-brake assembly may be located here. Remove the screw and nut at this location in either case.

The final rear fender connection is at the lower front portion of the fender. This spot is also tight, so a short or "L"-shaped screwdriver may be necessary. Remove this screw and nut, and lift the rear fender out of the frame.

Still More to Go

Many large parts are now off the frame, but a few of the small ones remain. What is still intact, however, is now much lighter and easier to move about. This is good, because the final disassembly is done with the bike in various positions.

Chain

Drive chain removal is nothing to be afraid of. The master, or connecting link, must be located first; it should be on the outboard side of the bicycle. Looking directly at the master link, place thumbs on the chain rivets on both sides of the master link. With remaining fingers on the backside of the chain, pull the chain (on both sides of master) back toward you, while pressing thumbs forward. The

Strike the stem bolt with a soft-faced hammer to dislodge the expansion wedge at the other end of the bolt.

Once the wedge is dislodged from the stem, pull the handlebar and stem assembly out with a pulling and twisting motion.

Loosen and remove the large nut atop the fork to separate the fork from the frame.

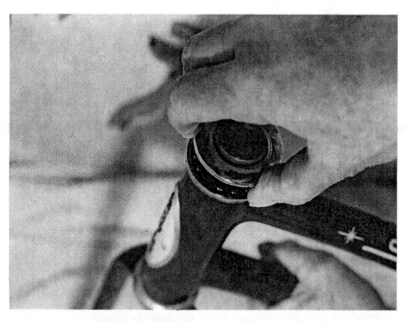

The bearing race/pre-load adjustment "nut" (cone) is threaded to the fork also, and must be spun off.

Handlebar Stem

Removing the handlebar stem from the fork tube is a simple operation, but only if you know the procedure. The first step is to loosen the bolt at the top of the stem. The large nut at the top of the fork tube does not affect this operation, as is often believed. Do not remove the stem bolt completely, just back it out about 1/4 inch.

Next, strike the bolt head with a soft-faced hammer, or with a steel hammer and a block of wood. What this does is dislodge the wedge at the bottom of the stem bolt from the split lower portion of the handlebar stem. With the wedge no longer in place, the expansion connection is released, allowing you to pull the handlebars and stem from the fork tube.

Make note of the relative positions of the bearings, nuts, and washer as you take the fork out of the frame.

goal is to bend the two pegs in the master link closer to each other, allowing the front of the master link to lift right off. The part being removed snaps into slots at the tops of the pegs.

Now the back of the master link (with the pegs) and the entire chain can be removed. To remove any other chain rivets or links, a special chain tool should be used. The tool needed is a chain rivet extractor. You must have this tool for chain removal if a chain has no master link, or if you add or subtract links.

Some left and right twisting, using the handlebars as leverage, may be necessary to get the stem out of the fork. In extreme cases, penetrating oil can be sprayed in the top (stem bolt must be removed) and bottom (through front fender screw hole) of the stem, and left to soak. Stubborn removal may also require putting the fork (protected with rags) in a vise to provide a firm hold, while twisting the stem back and forth. The inevitable presence of rust can create a challenge here—be patient.

Handlebars

You must loosen the bolt (sometimes with a nut) that tightens the stem clamp to hold the handlebars, to separate the stem from the bar. The clamp may need to be spread a bit to slide the bar out. You can use a broad-tipped screwdriver to spread the clamp, but do so cautiously. Applying too much force can permanently damage the stem and even leave micro cracks in an aluminum stem that may later lead to failure without warning.

Fork

Now loosen the nut at the top of the fork tube. Hold the fork still for this operation, using a piece of wood, or hammer handle, held between the lower fork prongs. If necessary, place the fork in a rag-padded vise for a stronger hold. Loosen this nut by turning it in a counterclockwise direction.

The nut is just a locknut for the upper bearing race/pre-load adjustment (adjusting cone). The bearing race is also threaded to the fork tube,

As the first step in tire removal, take off the valve cap (if it's there), and unscrew the valve stem core.

Bicycle tire irons work well, as they are designed to protect the tube and hook to the spokes to hold the bead off the rim for removal.

Push the valve stem up and out of the hole in the rim.

Carefully pull the tube from the tire, while holding the bead away from the rim.

The spoke/tube protector should be in one piece, and must be stretched slightly for removal. If it's broken or missing, replace it.

and must be spun off. Use fingers or groove-joint pliers (with some protection on the jaws) for this.

With the nut, washer, and bearing race removed, the fork should literally fall right out. Be sure to notice the position and direction of the bearings as you remove them. There is a top and bottom bearing, and a proper direction for each one. This will be discussed more during assembly. Remove the lower bearing race, if fork painting is required.

Seat Post

There is a bolt and nut either in the frame or in a clamp on the frame, which holds the seat post in place. This bolt and/or clamp narrows the gap of the slot in the frame tube when tightened, and lets the gap expand when loosened.

After you loosen this fastener, just pull the stem and seat assembly out of the frame. It will take some twisting back and forth, while pulling, using the seat as a handle.

In a stubborn case, to remove the seat from the post, place it in a vise (upside down), pour or squirt oil down the seat tube from inside the bottom bracket shell, and let it sit for 30 minutes. Then, carefully use the entire bike frame as a handle for twisting leverage.

Seat

Remove the seat from the stem by loosening the nut on the bolt that squeezes the seat-to-stem clamp.

Tires/Tubes

There is more information on tire and wheel assemblies in other chapters, but here is some basic information on removing tires and tubes from rims.

Valve stem caps are often missing, but remove them first if you have

39

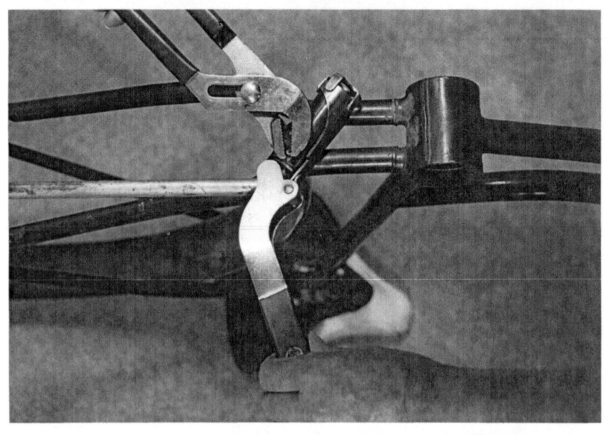

Use the special tool made for kickstand removal if you have it. Use leverage to compress the collar, and pull the retaining pin out.

them. Next unscrew the valve stem core with a suitable tool. This will let all of the air out of the tube and makes removing the tube easier.

If you have bicycle tire irons, now is the time to use them. Tire irons are generally in sets of three. They are designed with rounded edges so the chance of damaging a tube is minimal; most tire irons also have slots that can be hooked to the spokes to hold the tire bead off the rim. If you don't have tire irons (and you should, they're cheap enough), dull, flat-bladed screwdrivers can be used in a pinch. If screwdrivers are used, take extra care not to poke, pinch, or puncture the tube. Factory shop manuals say not to use screwdrivers, but in the real world, they do the job if used very carefully.

Use large groove-joint pliers (with a rag to protect paint) to depress the collar enough to allow the pin (pointed at with screwdriver) to be pulled out.

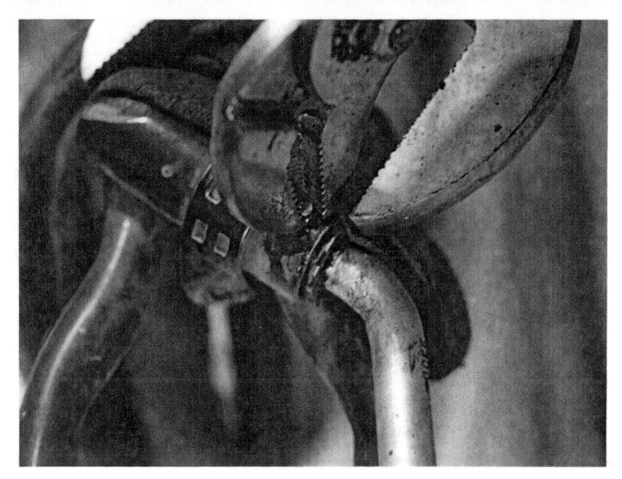

Use another set of pliers to pull the retaining pin out, while the collar (on right in photo) is depressed with large pliers.

Start at any point on the tire, use the tire iron to pry the tire bead up and over the edge of the rim, then hook the tire iron on a spoke to hold it in place. Use a second and third iron to continue prying the bead over the rim, all around the circumference. After about halfway around the rim, you can pull the bead on one side of the tire away from the rim by hand.

When one side of the tire is completely off the rim, push the valve stem up and out of the hole in the rim. Now pull the tube out of the tire here, and all around the rim, while holding the tire bead away from the rim. Do this carefully, as the tube is often stuck to the tire or rim.

Slide the kickstand and spring out of the tube after you have pulled the retaining pin through the hole and out of the collar groove (on right in photo).

41

Bearing cups shown from the backside after removal. The wooden broom handle and/or the seat stem absorb the damage from the removal blows and protect the cups.

Remove the tire now, by pulling the remaining bead away from the rim by hand. Remove from the same side of the rim that the first bead and tube were pulled from.

The one-piece spoke/tube protection band should be in place circling the rim and covering the spoke nipples. Remove it by stretching the band over the edge of the rim, and off. If the band is broken or missing, it must be replaced before reassembly.

Kickstand

The kickstand is commonly located right behind the crank, although a few very old bikes use a U-shaped stand connected to the rear hub. Normal, side kickstands are either bolted on or mounted in a tube that is welded to the frame.

If you have a bolt-on kickstand, simply remove the nut and bolt from the clamp to get it off. If you have the model that is in a welded tube, removal appears intimidating, but you can do it. There is a special tool available at bike shops that makes this job easy—if you plan on more than one restoration, it's a worthwhile purchase.

A large pair of groove-joint pliers is another tool that works well for removing these Schwinn-type kickstands (if your frame is not going to be painted, and the kickstand works, you do not have to remove it). The collar on the kickstand side of the tube must be pressed in (against

spring tension) just slightly, to allow the pin (see photo) to be pulled out. While the collar is depressed, pull out the small retaining pin with another set of pliers. With the retaining pin out, slide the kickstand, collar, and spring right out of the tube. There is also a position cam within the frame tube. If you wish to remove it, tap it out with a screwdriver or punch from the sprocket side. There is more discussion of these kickstands in chapter 5. The revived Schwinn bicycle company produces a number of "retro" bikes and replacement parts, including these kickstands.

The bolt-on kickstands are located in the same area as the welded tube style, which is directly behind the

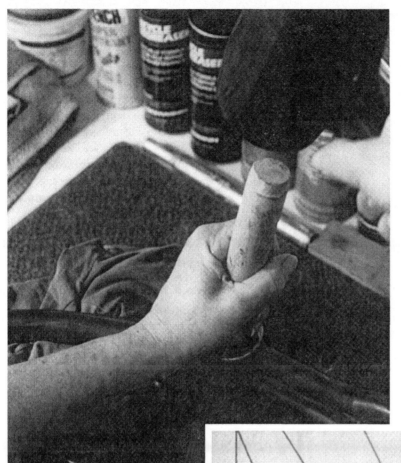

crank. If your bicycle has no kickstand, it most likely once had a bolt-on style. You can easily find an accurate replacement in most bike shops.

Bearing Cups

Removing bearing cups looks intimidating, but it's actually easy. If the bike will not be painted, and if cups are in good shape, you can even leave them in place. Cleaning and reconditioning of these parts, however, as with all parts, is easier when you have removed them from the bike.

For the crank-bearing cups, place the frame on its side. Position the frame on a rag-covered block of wood, so that the bottom-bearing cup is off the floor or workbench surface. This will allow the cup that is now on the bottom to be tapped out with a hammer and your tool of choice. Use a hard piece of wood (like a piece of broom handle), an old aluminum seat

With the tool placed against the backside lip of the bearing cup, strike the tool with the hammer. Move the tool from one side of the cup to the other, and strike until the cup drops out.

Position the frame so that the fork tube cup to be removed is off of the work surface and the frame rests on a covered wooden block. Strike the backside lip of the cup with a chosen tool and hammer.

Most original braces are riveted on. If they are to be removed, you must drill the rivets out from the backside.

When drilling the rivets, just drill lightly to remove rivet material, being careful not to drill through the brace.

post, or a brass drift for this operation. Don't use a hard steel punch, or you'll damage the edges of the bearing cups.

Place the tool against the lip of the bearing cup from its backside, make sure everything is stable, and take a good strike with the hammer. It may require a few hits, alternating to various positions around the lip of the cup, to knock out the cup. Repeat the procedure for the remaining crank-bearing cup.

You can pound out fork tube-bearing cups the same way. Again, position the frame on a rag-covered block of wood, so the cup to be removed is off of the work surface. Place the tool against the backside of the bearing cup, and strike the tool with a hammer, moving the tool around the perimeter of the cup. Then turn the frame over and repeat this procedure for the second fork tube cup.

Reflectors

Reflectors come in many sizes and styles, and many are shown throughout this book. Most attach to the bike in the same way, however, with one or two nuts holding most reflectors from the backside of the fender. Some are held with hex nuts, some with flex nuts, and some older ones are attached to a riveted bracket on the fender.

Typically, unscrew the fender reflector by hand, while holding the nut on the inside of the fender with a small wrench or pliers. Some older reflectors are quite unique, and care should be taken when removing them from your bike.

Reflectors, whether original or accessory, often appear in many other locations on a bicycle. These can be about any size or shape, and are usually threaded stud mount, clip mount (pry-off removal), or glued on.

Certain head badges are attached with small pegs. Pry these small pegs out with a sturdy knife blade to remove the badge. Be careful, because you risk damaging the badge, especially if it's a thin, tin head badge.

Fender Braces

Original fender braces are commonly riveted in place. If the fender and braces will be reused intact, removing the braces is not necessary. If the fender needs rolling (for dents), painting, or new braces, drill the rivets out from backside.

Other Parts and Pieces

There is still some remaining hardware on the bicycle frame. Take all of this off before you begin cleaning, painting, or mechanical restoration.

Remove the seat clamp from the frame by hand with a twisting motion. For a tight one, you will have to spread the clamp with a prying tool.

Spread the coaster brake lever clamp by hand, and remove it from the frame.

Some head badges are held on with screws and come off easily. For badges attached with rivet-type pegs, pry the rivets out with a knife or chisel. As with so many other parts, if removing them is too difficult, and original paint is retained, taking them off may not be necessary.

Now that the bicycle is in pieces, the remaining process of restoration can begin.

Some head badges are affixed with screws for easy removal.

45

CHAPTER 5

Mechanical Restoration

The mechanical portion of the average collector bicycle consists of very few actual moving parts. The relative simplicity of bicycles compared to automobiles or motorcycles is one factor in their continuous user demand. This popularity is not lost on collectors either, since a bike's mechanical restoration is not too complex.

The basic moving parts of a bike are ball-bearing equipped, and include the crank, pedals, fork, front hub, and rear hub. You can service these systems with average mechanical skills and a few tips. The only exception to self-service might be the rear hub, which you may, depending on your skills, wish to take to a professional bicycle mechanic. This is especially true when dealing with coaster brakes, two-speed kickback hubs, and three-speed planetary hubs. Learning about them is fun and interesting, but if you don't want to take on the project, take the hub to a mechanic. It'll save time and frustration and really won't cost all that much.

While the ball-bearing portions of a bicycle are very important to its smooth operation, some other mechanical parts need servicing also. These parts include the spokes/rims, kickstand, and on some models, hand-operated brakes. As always, follow manufacturers' safety recommendations for use of tools and handling of chemicals and solvents.

Front Hub

Conventional front hubs consist of a set of bearings, adjustable

For rear hub service, you might consider taking the hub to a bicycle mechanic. Tackle it yourself if you are mechanically confident, but try to get an exploded parts diagram first. Every hub is unique, and each one has many small pieces, so disassemble them carefully.

Front hubs are very basic, consisting of an axle, bearings, adjustable cones, and locknuts.

The inside view of an Atom-brand expander-brake backing plate reveals the shoes and springs within. This is a simple, cable-operated unit.

cones, locknuts, a threaded axle, and a main shell. The axle passes through the hub shell and is affixed to the front fork. The wheel and hub rotate around the axle, riding on ball bearings to reduce friction. One variation is that some hubs have removable races, or bearing cups, and others have races integral to the hub housing. The ramification of this is that if the surface of an integral race is badly pitted or worn, you will have to replace the entire hub. You might also run across a front hub with an expander brake. This hub is larger in diameter than a conventional hub, so as to include a brake drum. A backing plate with the expandable shoes is affixed to the axle, and has an external lever to actuate the brake mechanism.

Some collector bikes were also equipped with front hubs that included a built-in generator. If these need electrical repair, it may require more expertise than you have or even more than what your local bike shop can offer. You might try finding a local electrical shop to help you with this unique hub.

Hold the bearing cone still, while rotating the front-axle locknut counterclockwise to remove it.

Spin the locknut and the bearing cone one at a time, off of the axle to reveal the bearing. If you need to hold the other end of the axle for this, be sure to protect the threads.

If your hub has a locknut outside the bearing cone (most do), remove it first. Do not try to spin the cone and the locknut off together, as that will damage the threads. This is where to use your thin hub wrench to fit in the narrow gap between the locknut and the hub. Hold the bearing cup with the appropriate hub wrench, and rotate the locknut counterclockwise (when viewed from the end of the axle toward locknut) to break it loose. Continue to rotate the locknut all the way off of the axle. You may need to hold the axle with pliers, while protecting the axle threads by some means. At your local bike shop, mechanics usually hold the axle in a copper jaw vise. You can use a rag, rubber or copper tubing, or even a couple pennies to protect the threads from pliers, locking pliers, or vise jaws. Now rotate the bearing cone off of the axle. With the locknut and bearing cone off of one side of the axle, slide the bearing set (sometimes loose balls) off, and pull the axle from the hous-

ing. Take the remaining bearing set off the other end of the axle, noting the direction of placement. The remaining locknut and bearing cone can stay in place, if replacement is not necessary, and axle was centered before removal.

Inspect all pieces for damage (pitted bearings or bearing contact surfaces, bent axle, or stripped threads) to determine if replacement is necessary. If the hub has removable bearing cups, leave them in place if they are not worn or pitted. If there is an expander brake, remove the entire brake backing plate (with shoes and springs intact) by taking off the axle locknut. New Old Stock front hubs are available for reasonable prices, but replacement requires re-lacing of rims and spokes. Now is the time to degrease and clean the hub if you are reusing it. Scrub the hub-to-spoke area and entire hub with a toothbrush and solvent (degreaser). Clean these areas with a rag, then finish by blowing off the residue with compressed air or a quick drying aerosol cleaner

After a complete cleaning, your front hub should be spotless. Check the inner bearing race for wear; some are removable, but most are integral to the hub. If the inner cup (race) is pitted or badly worn, replace the hub.

There are a lot of rear hub variations. Even this single speed Bendix coaster brake model has a lot of internal parts.

Many muscle bikes, like the Krate series, use a freewheeling derailleur-style gear cluster.

(brake or electrical cleaner). See rear hub cleaning photos.

Rear Hub

One bicycle dealer service manual covering 1946 through 1969 bicycles contains 350 pages covering rear hubs. There are so many rear hub designs that it is impossible to cover them all here. Common brands are Morrow, Peerless, New Departure, Bendix, and Sturmey-Archer. The various makes represent one-, two-, three-, and four-speed rear hubs, with and without coaster brakes. Many of the muscle-type bikes (like Sting-Rays) of the late 1960s use a free-wheeling derailleur rear gear (sprocket) cluster.

Servicing any of these rear hubs requires good mechanical aptitude, special tools in some cases, and knowledge of the hub's workings, along with great care and patience. If you possess all these attributes and virtues, you can probably service a single-speed hub, at least. Even with a single speed, it's best to have an exploded diagram of the hub you are working on as a guide. A two-, three-, or four-speed hub has enough small pieces (springs, pawls, balls, keys, etc.) to discourage even those of us who feel mechanically adept.

A rear hub is basically designed like a front hub, with a threaded axle, sporting locknuts, and adjustable bearing cones at both ends. It's all

those parts (about 30 to 50) in the middle that can get you in trouble. If you want to disassemble and service a rear hub, it is highly recommended (again) that you find an exploded diagram to guide you. These can be found in factory service manuals (sometimes a bike shop will copy one for you), and some are posted in various places on the Internet. The best thing, in most cases, is to have your rear hub serviced by a professional bicycle mechanic.

Certain hubs have a capped hole at their center, to which you can add a bit of oil. You can also back off the locknuts and bearing cones, and inject grease into the outer bearings in a pinch. Be careful when doing

49

These are the many internal parts of a manual-shift Bendix two-speed hub. It's easy to see why an exploded diagram, showing parts positions, is an important aid to reassembly.

To clean the rear hub (or front hub), first spray degreaser on dirty surfaces.

Thoroughly scrub the hub, sprocket, and spoke surfaces to remove grease, grit, and grime.

Blast the surfaces with compressed air to remove residue, and dry the area.

Use rubber gloves while scrubbing the bearings with a toothbrush and solvent. Degreaser or thinner works well for this. The plastic tub is cut out of the bottom of a one-gallon plastic container.

Blast bearings with compressed air after cleaning them to remove solvent and grit.

Your bearings and related components for the fork, crank, and front hub should be totally spotless after cleaning. They may be lubricated now, or just prior to assembly. Either way, protect and identify them by putting them in labeled, resealable sandwich bags until you're ready for them.

this, however, as allowing the axle to slide one way or the other will allow the internal parts to move out of place. If you have a totally seized rear hub, consider getting a replacement. As with the front hub, replacement of the rear hub will require re-lacing spokes and rims.

If you can reuse your rear hub, carefully clean the exterior of the hub assembly with degreaser. Use a toothbrush to scrub all of it, especially the sprocket area, where grease and grit accumulate. Dissolve and brush all the grime, and finish by blowing it clean and dry with compressed air or aerosol cleaner.

Bearing Cleaning and Inspection

Clean all bearings, bearing retainers, cups, and adjustable cones from the hub, crank, and headset. The old grease is probably hard or waxy; dissolve it with degreaser, mineral spirits, thinner, or other suitable solvent. Use rubber gloves when working with these solvents to avoid skin irritation. Scrub the bearings with a toothbrush to dislodge the old grease and dirt. Dry the parts with a rag, and finish cleaning with a blast of compressed air if you have it. Aerosol products like brake and electrical cleaners work well for blowing off the last bits of contamination, and dry as well as compressed air, because of their rapid evaporation characteristics.

Inspect bearings for pitting and wear. Check separate balls on a flat table for roundness. You can buy new ones by their diameter at most bike shops. Test retained ball bearings as a set, by rotating the clean and dry set in its companion-bearing cup. Movement should be smooth, even without grease, if there is no contamination or excess wear present. Closely inspect all bearing cups and cones for wear patterns also. It is normal to have a visible, slightly worn path or groove where the bearings ride. It is not good to have pitting or irregular wear, however. Even though loads are not great on bicycle bearings, replace irregular or pitted bearings, cups, or cones (races) with new ones, or better ones from a parts bike. You can buy complete (bearings, cones, and cups) headsets and crank sets from classic bike catalog suppliers for reasonable prices. Place cleaned bearings in labeled plastic sandwich bags to identify and protect the parts until you lube and install them. If assembly is a long way off, it's a good idea to pre-lube the bearings before storing.

Bearing Lubrication

This operation will get your hands greasy, but it's nice clean grease. Use rubber or latex gloves if you wish, but the best way to lube bearings in retainers is to apply the grease with your fingers. This allows you to sort of press the grease into the retainers, and to spread grease evenly where you want it. Use high-quality grease designed for bicycle bearings, available at any bike shop. This grease comes in a one-pound tub (about a pint), or can also be found in a tube, which allows you to "inject" the grease where needed. Grease all bearing surfaces and ball/retainer assemblies with a liberal coat of the high temperature bicycle lubricating grease. Bearings from the bottom bracket (crank), headset (fork tube), and hubs need this type of lube.

Chain

Chains are usually the first part to wear out on a bicycle's drivetrain. If heavily used or "stretched," a badly worn chain can ruin chain rings and cogs. Although it might be difficult to find a replacement for those

Use your fingers to press grease into bearing retainers, and coat the entire bearing surface.

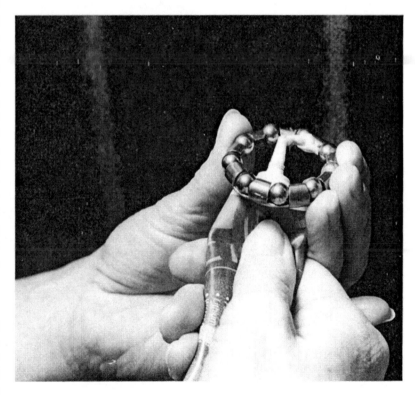

With grease from a tube, you can inject the lube into retainers, but coat the outer surface as well.

For degreasing and cleaning, soak the chain in a suitable container with degreaser or solvent. It will take some time to dissolve old caked-on grease, and probably some scrubbing with a brush. As usual, compressed air helps in the final cleaning.

A chain rivet tool like this must be used for modifying (shortening or lengthening) any chain, or for removing one without a master link. See chapter 4 for its operation.

increasingly rare 1-inch skip chains, it may be worth it. If you find a good source, buy a couple.

Either way, your drive chain will probably need degreasing, or be dry and rusty. If you're lucky, your chain can be reused after you clean and lubricate it. For degreasing, soak the chain in a suitable container, in which you can cover the chain with degreaser, solvent, or thinner. Citrus degreasers are a bit less toxic and worth a try also. Nonetheless, use rubber gloves when working around any solvent.

After a good soaking, use a toothbrush to scrub the dirt and old hardened grease from the chain (wear gloves). Blow off any residue, and dry the chain with compressed air or aerosol cleaner. Spray the chain heavily with penetrant or lubricant (Liquid Wrench or WD-40), and wrap the chain in a rag to await final lubrication and assembly. When it's time to attach the chain, lubricate it thoroughly but lightly. Clean off the

Some older pedals are designed to come apart, while many are not. Even the ones that aren't can be disassembled if necessary, with some ingenuity. These pedals have flattened threads to keep the nuts on, which have to be filed for disassembly. You can lube the bearings with a squirt of oil, however, leaving the pedal intact.

excess, because too much lubricant defeats the purpose by attracting dirt. Your chain will need to be wiped off and lubricated regularly.

If you replace your chain or modify its length, you'll need to use a chain rivet tool. These tools are designed to easily push chain rivets in and out without damage.

Pedals

If your pedals are seized on their shafts, look for some replacements. Most bicycle pedals are difficult to take apart, but it is possible. Depending on the manufacturer, some are tougher to disassemble than others. The long screws running through the pedal blocks might be meant to stay there, because of their smooth heads and threads that are flattened to keep the nuts in place. With some filing or grinding you can still take them apart, but you might destroy the screws. There are inner and outer bearings on pedals, and if you can't get them apart easily, squirt some oil or other lubricant in the crack where they spin.

New old stock and excellent reproduction pedals are available, and may be the easiest way to go. Old pedals that rotate freely, and still have decent rubber, are good to reuse also. If you want to retain the aged look, and your pedal rubber is missing, you might make one good pedal out of two bad ones. To do that, you will have to take them apart, so study your pedals carefully to see if you can. If your pedals come apart, you can also buy new rubber blocks from vintage parts suppliers. Pedals are natural items to find on a parts bike. Remember—pedals are threaded differently for left and right sides, so be sure you have one of each if you mix and match. The metal portion of the

pedals can be cosmetically improved (see chapter 6), but the outside area of most used pedals is normally a bit rough, as it's the first thing to hit the ground when a bike is laid down. The earlier vintage pedals disassemble easier than the later ones, but if you're creative, you can get any of them apart.

Kickstand

The older bikes (1940s and earlier) have swing-type kickstands, attached near the rear hub. Because of their simple design, if they are not missing, they probably work fine. The trouble spot with the swing-type stand is often a missing spring clip retainer. The retainer is

Many of the very old bikes have a swing-type rear stand, which attaches at the rear hub. These are a pretty trouble-free setup, and if they aren't missing, should work great. A rear fender clip holds the stand in the up position for riding, and is available from specialty suppliers if needed.

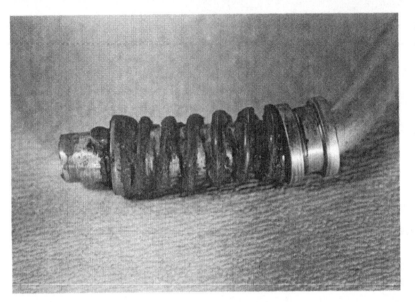

You can remove this built-in Schwinn kickstand by more than one method (see chapter 4). If it sags, so the crank hits it when you pedal, or it rotates forward, allowing the bike to fall, inspect the parts. A broken pin can be replaced, as well as a loose or broken spring. Aftermarket suppliers or parts bikes are good sources.

This cam is located in the frame tube and controls the kickstand positions. If it is damaged, replace it.

attached to the rear fender and holds the stand in the up position for riding. This part's popularity makes it readily available from vintage parts suppliers.

Schwinn developed a built-in kickstand in 1946, with a tube welded to the frame, housing an integral sprag (kickstand and spring assembly). This style of kickstand is a simple design and removes easily (see chapter 4). If your kickstand of this type hangs too low in the up position, or folds forward allowing the bike to tip, replacement is indicated. Again, this is a common problem, so you can buy a new sprag (kickstand and spring) from any of the old bike parts suppliers. The sag, or looseness, is caused by a weak or broken spring, a broken spring retaining a pin, or by a damaged cam within the frame tube. If your spring is fine, but the spring retaining pin is broken, get a new pin from a fastener specialist. Parts bikes are a good source for kickstand parts also. Finally, a rarer problem is a damaged positioning stop (cam) within the frame tube. If the spring and pin are okay, and the kickstand won't stay in the up or down position, inspect this part. Replace the cam by tapping it out of the frame tube with a hammer and punch and dropping in a new one. When you install the cam, notice the slash mark(s) on the outside end, denoting the bottom of the part.

A third style kickstand is designed like the Schwinn type, but the entire assembly bolts to the frame via a clamp setup. Like the integral type, sag or looseness is best corrected by replacement. Parts bikes and vintage suppliers are good sources for these. Check for matching length when you are searching for a replacement.

If you replace the cam, be sure that the slash mark is positioned to the bottom of the bike.

Rims and Spokes

A very bent or badly dented rim is not worth saving. New old stock, reproduction, and good used rims are plentiful. If your hubs are usable, you can lace (re-spoke) them to the replacement rims. When painting or plating a rim, you must remove the spokes also. Lacing (installing spokes) or truing a rim is another operation (like rear hub service) that you may want to let a professional bike mechanic handle. They already have the experience and practice it takes to be good at lacing and truing, but you can master these operations too, if you take the time.

Lacing a hub to a rim with spokes is like solving a puzzle. Have a complete wheel on hand as a guide, before attempting spoke placement. The spokes are secured to the rim with threaded nipples, which are removed by screwing them off the ends of the spokes. During general disassembly, you should have removed the tire, tube, and rubber rim band from the rim. Remove the spoke nipples by unscrewing each one from its spoke. Take each spoke out of the hub as its nipple is removed. Before lacing, make sure the replacement rim has the same total number of spoke holes as the hub (36 is common), and that it is the proper diameter. Replace the spokes in their original configuration in the hub and rim, and secure with the spoke nipples.

Spokes are actually part of a bicycle's suspension, as they flex and absorb shock. The spokes also control the straightness of the rim they support. A straight, evenly tensioned rim assembly is one of the most important aspects of a good riding bike. Whether you have just laced the rim, or you have an existing assembly, you or a pro must tension the spokes and

A spoke wrench is the recommended tool for spoke adjustment. It is designed to turn the spoke nipples without doing damage to them.

57

true the rim. With an understanding of the basic truing principles, along with practice, you can do it.

It's best to practice truing operations on an old wheel to get a feel for it. You should have a spoke wrench for turning the nipples. Spoke wrenches come in single sizes to fit your bike, or multi-sized versions for a universal fit. If the tire is off of the rim, you can use a screwdriver to turn the nipples from the tire side of the rim. With the tire in place, a spoke wrench is mandatory and usually preferred by the pros whether the tire is on or off, because of the superior grip of the spoke wrench on the adjustable nipples. Never use pliers or adjustable wrenches, as they will scuff, round, and eventually weaken the nipples. Replace all such damaged nipples, and any missing or broken spokes. If you cannot turn some of the nipples, apply penetrating oil to loosen them. To remove absolutely frozen nipples, cut the spoke, and replace with a new spoke and nipple. You must be able to turn all of the nipples to properly tension the wheel. As earlier mentioned, don't try to work with an out-of-round, severely bent, or dented rim.

Always use some sort of thread treatment on spokes and nipples before assembly. The Swiss company DT makes a nice spoke compound that not only lubricates the threads for assembly, but then dries to firmly hold them in place after the wheel has been trued.

A truing stand is great for this operation, but as usual, shouldn't be purchased unless you're going to work on many bikes. An alternative to using a truing stand is using an old front fork mounted in a vise, or truing the wheels while in the bike (upside down). Use chalk or a felt-tip marker to mark areas out of true, as you slowly spin the wheel. By tightening

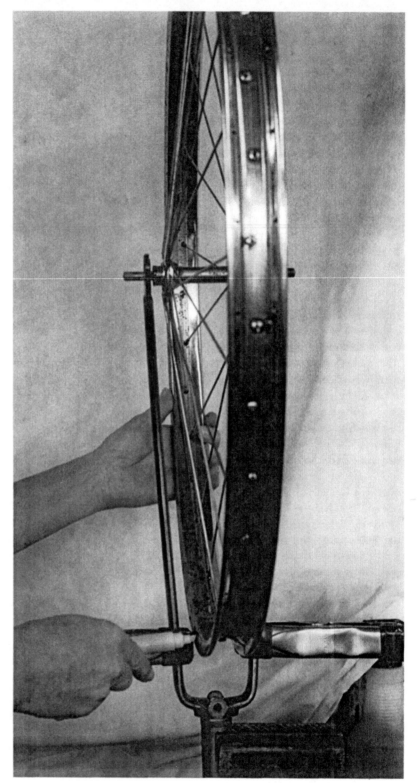

Use a marker or chalk for making reference marks while truing a rim.

A professional truing stand works great if you have one, but you can fashion one by using an old fork and a vise. Truing the wheels while they are on the bicycle is also a possibility.

and loosening spokes, you will adjust the lateral (side-to-side) runout (wobble), and vertical irregularity (low or high spots) of the rim. You can do lateral corrections with the tire in place, but you must have the tire off for any vertical adjustment. If you are doing the truing in the midst of your restoration process, the tires should be off anyway, but you can fine-tune the lateral adjustment even after the bike is fully assembled.

Snug the loosest spokes first, and attempt to get all the spoke tensions about equal, but not too tight. A tool called a spoke tensionometer exists, but many pros don't even have one, so you must develop a feel for spoke tension. Pluck the spokes with a fingernail, or tap them with a metal object (like a screwdriver) to hear the audible tone of each spoke (higher for tight, lower for loose). Observe the number of spoke threads showing on the hub side of the nipple as another indication of spoke tension. In equalizing spoke tension, you may even loosen some of the tightest ones to begin with. You will become good at this if you're willing to practice.

With the spoke tension equalized, the rim should already be straighter than when you started. As you spin the rim past a reference point, mark (using a marker or chalk) the biggest lateral runout (wobble) to begin with. The basic principle to correct a wobble is to loosen the spokes connected to one side of the hub, and tighten those on the other side. Again, it is only through practice that you will get the feel for this. Continue to spin the rim, marking and adjusting the crooked areas from the biggest to the smallest. The vertical adjustment (when a wheel is out-of-round) is not as common, but uses the same principle of tightening and

Hand-operated caliper-type brakes appear on some muscle bikes, and a few other models. There is not much to servicing them, other than cable adjustment and rubber pad replacement.

loosening. However, instead of involving spokes left and right of one another, it involves spokes 180 degrees apart and across from one another. If you have a rear hub where the spokes are shorter on the right than on the left (like a derailleur gear set), spoke tension is higher on the right than the left.

Wheel truing is definitely a learned art. If you don't feel comfortable with it, or if a complete re-lacing is needed, consider one of the local professionals. Mechanics in bike shops do this every day and have the experience through their practice to do it quickly and well. It's also fun to try to get good at it yourself, once you know the basics, so now it's up to you.

Hand Brakes

Hand-actuated, lever/cable-operated brakes are used on certain models. These can be expanding-shoe drum brakes or caliper-type, rim brakes. There is not much to servicing them, other than cable adjustment. Parts you should check for wear are the shoes (friction material) on drum-type brakes and the rubber pads on the caliper-type brakes. Broken cables are also common, which you must replace. Of all the bikes in the collector category, only a small percentage use this type of brake. The exceptions are the muscle bikes (like the Krate series), which use caliper brakes because their derailleur rear hubs preclude use of coaster brakes.

Expander-type drum brakes also require cable adjustment and occasional shoe (friction material) replacement.

Tires and Tubes

Tire and tubes are as much a cosmetic as a mechanical consideration in your restoration. The main mechanical aspect is whether or not they will hold air. First, if an old tube has one hole in it, a patch is probably okay. Put some air in the tube, and immerse it in a bucket of water to check for leaks (air bubbles). If a tube already has some patches, or has more than one hole, buy a new tube. Also, if the rim band is broken (it should be a contin-uous, unbroken band) or missing, replace it. Both the tube and the rim band are inexpensive and are readily available at bicycle shops. Be sure to buy the exact size to fit your tire.

Old bicycle tires usually have some cracks in the sidewalls. You can still use these tires, if they will hold the pressure of a tube filled with air. If you plan to ride your restored bike much, however, find tires with small, few, or no cracks. The problem with the cracks is that as you ride and the tire flexes, the cracks will enlarge and let the tube blow out through the hole. Also make sure you find tires of the correct size and design for your bike. Schwinn rims, for example, use a unique "straight line" rim requiring a special tire bead to fit right. Even though your bike came with a certain brand tire, there are many manufac-turers to select from, including repro-ductions. Vintage suppliers, hobbyists, the Internet, and bicycle shops are all good sources for tires.

CHAPTER 6

Cosmetic Restoration

Required Tools
- Steel wool ("00" or "000")
- Abrasive cleaner/polish
- Wax/sealer
- Rubber cleaner
- All-purpose cleaner
- Brushes, nylon and brass
- Flat file
- Rags
- Goggles
- Rubber gloves

Recommended Tools
- Compressed air
- Silver aerosol paint (chrome or aluminum)
- Aerosol vinyl dye
- Touch-up paint
- Body shop dollies or access to fender roller

With your bicycle in pieces, you must now use your judgment and ingenuity to improve each individual piece. Using the "whole is the sum of its parts" concept, concentrate on one part at a time, restoring its condition as much as possible. In this way, you will end up with the ingredients to reassemble a complete bike of which to be proud.

Chromed Pieces

Most bicycles have fine chrome plating on pieces such as handlebars, stem (gooseneck), sprocket, crank, and other small parts. Many bicycles also have chromed fenders, rims, and accessories (racks, tanks, etc.), while some even have a chrome frame. The trouble is, after years, this fine chrome usually looks pretty bad. One of the most amazing aspects of bicycle restoration is how well you can bring these factory-chromed parts back from their deteriorated state.

You will transform parts that initially look far-gone to a nearly new look with some effort. Most of the contamination appearing on these parts is surface rust, which, most often, you can remove. Start the process by spraying the chrome with a spray lubricant or penetrating oil. Next, grab some of your fine 00 or 000 steel wool, which is one of your main restoration "tools."

Use rubber gloves while rubbing and polishing with fine steel wool, because it breaks into slivers, which end up lodged in unprotected fingers. This fine polishing steel wool works wonders for removing surface rust and other stubborn chrome contamination. There are other material

This rear hub area is typical of an old bike.

After disassembly, degreasing, and other restoration of each small piece, the assembled final product is dramatically improved.

Old neglected chrome pieces suffer from rust and other contamination.

Some work with steel wool and a brass brush will restore this old chrome rim to new condition.

options such as brass wool, bronze wool, or synthetic scrubbers, which you may use, but most restorers use steel wool. The important factor is the "fineness" of the product. If you use anything besides 00 or 000 steel wool, test to make sure it doesn't scratch the chrome.

Using plenty of pressure, and even some chrome cleaner or polish if desired, rub the parts until they sparkle like new. Have a rag handy to wipe the surface, and check your progress occasionally; you don't want to rub any more than is necessary to remove the rust and corrosion. Use a toothbrush-sized brass-bristled brush in slots, crevices or knurled areas on rims. Use compressed air to blow away tiny bits of steel wool that might be left in pores or small pits. Finish off all cleaned parts with wax (straight carnauba is best) to seal and protect from reformation of rust.

If, after cleaning this way, you have parts with peeling, badly pitted, or missing chrome, replacement or re-plating is the only remedy. For re-chroming, the only preparation necessary is to save up some money before you head to the metal-plating shop. Re-chroming is very expensive, so shop around to compare prices, and consider replacement parts if you can find them. Sometimes a bit of silver paint applied to bad spots will allow you to live with a part until you find a replacement.

63

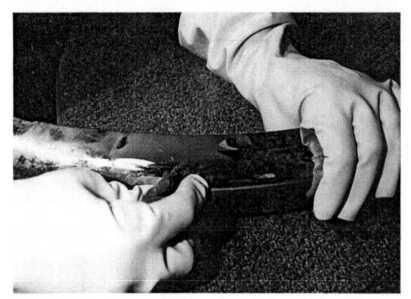

Good old "chrome" silver (shinier) or aluminum (duller) spray paint works wonders to touch up these other plated parts, but not necessarily by spraying them. First, wash and thoroughly dry all of the parts. Usually there will just be portions of the part (bottom of kickstand, ends of pedals, inside of fender braces) that have deteriorated. There is a restoration "trick" to use on these parts that works well. Spray the paint liberally on a paper towel, and rub the paint on the affected part. The deteriorated portions are a bit rough compared to the rest of the surface, and the paint sticks to these areas while blending with the original surface nicely. The part may not look perfect, but it will blend in well on an original bicycle. Typically, experimentation and experience will enhance your technique. Use your creativity in this and other ways to make each individual part of your bike the best it can be.

continued on page 81

Use rubber gloves when polishing chrome with fine steel wool. Otherwise you may end up with tiny steel slivers in your fingers.

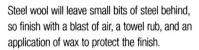

Steel wool will leave small bits of steel behind, so finish with a blast of air, a towel rub, and an application of wax to protect the finish.

Other Plated Pieces

Some bicycle parts, such as fender braces, pedal hardware, and kickstands, are cadmium or nickel plated. This kind of plating really looks a bit like silver paint. Restoration supply specialists (Eastwood Company) sell specific aerosol paints, so you can duplicate these finishes by sanding and repainting the parts. Metal-plating businesses also can re-plate these parts. If you are keeping your bike original, there is a good touchup method for these parts.

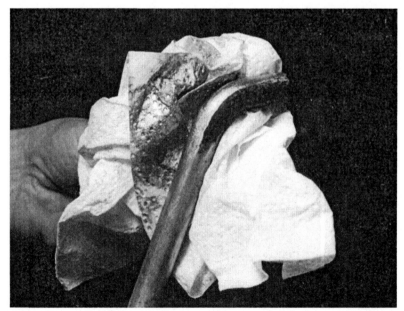

When you rub the paint on the part, the paint sticks to the unplated portions, and blends in the rest nicely.

How to Restore Your Collector Bicycle
PHOTO GALLERY

These bicycles were built more than 25 years before these girls were born, but they are fully functional after restoration (the bikes, not the girls).

This circa-1960 Schwinn holds a prominent position, as it adorns its owner's garage in lieu of immediate restoration.

Although these old Schwinns do not really fit most definitions of "antique," these shops regularly carry collector bikes like these. You may have to barter for a good price; shop in the winter when demand is lower.

After buying the Excelsior Motorcycle Company, Schwinn used the name on its bicycle badges for quite a while. This one beautifies the head tube of Kathy Bruce's 1950 Red Phantom.

The silver undercoat (and the primer, for that matter) is revealed on this candy apple red 1960 Schwinn Speedster. This happened during years of carrying the canvas saddlebags for a boy's newspaper route. That's a built-in history, or what some call "patina."

It just wouldn't be right to mess with the paint on a tank like this. If it looks this good after cleaning and polishing, ignore the few scratches, and leave it be.

Greg's 1966 Schwinn Sting-Ray Super Deluxe model includes factory goodies like a chromed and painted chain guard, bow pedals, whitewall knobby tires, and a bobbed rear fender treatment.

Schwinn's circa-1930 patented spring fork design is another feature that the factory has blended into the Super Deluxe.

Some parts don't come cheap. The chain guard for this 1937 Dayton Super Streamline is worth a few hundred dollars. Dave is still gathering parts for this one, but he had the crank and sprocket re-plated already.

The deluxe teardrop reflector, with the Schwinn "S" is used on premium models, such as Corvette, Jaguar, and tandems. If you find a good one, get it even if you don't need it, because they are good trading stock.

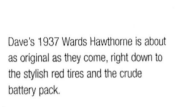

Dave's 1937 Wards Hawthorne is about as original as they come, right down to the stylish red tires and the crude battery pack.

In a quest to be different, The Evans Company used squared (side-to-side), rather than curved, fenders on this Colson model.

The 1954 heavyweight Jaguar was about the last of the breed with a 2.125-inch tire, as Schwinn introduced middleweights this same year. The factory-installed lever/cable-operated three-speed hub is rare on a heavy model like this.

Mike's 1953 Green Panther is in very desirable original condition. It does have enough value to sustain the cost of a total restoration, however, if the owner was so inclined.

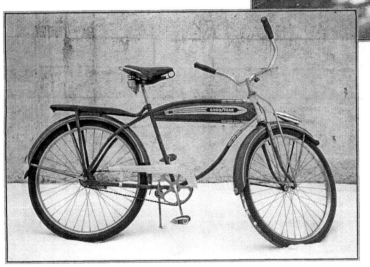

Tire manufacturers evidently wanted to sell bikes, as well as tires over the years. This mid-1950s Goodyear model sports the company logo proudly on the tank and head badge and, of course, the tires.

Everyone likes original bikes, and that is why the owner of this 1936 Excelsior Schwinn is so proud of it. That red rubber on the tires, grips, and pedals looks outstanding!

Schwinn Phantoms made many kids happy during the 1950s. This was the company's top of the line, and they are not all black. Phantoms came in red, like this one, along with green, and ever-popular black.

Willard chose custom colors to paint his 1954 J.C. Higgins Deluxe when he restored it, but those colors sure look like they belong there.

For the restoration of the 1948 J.C. Higgins, Willard used the original color scheme. You won't see many skirt guards (louvered covers at the rear tire), but now you know what they look like.

"Three-of-a-kind" (almost). They are all 1961 blue Schwinn Tornados with ivory rims and graphics, but they differ a bit. On top is a stock 26-inch model, in the middle is a 24-inch version with a custom seat and handgrips, and at the bottom is a 20-inch "Sting-Rayized" bike with an accessory banana seat, high bars, and streamers.

These 1962 Schwinn middleweights belonged to brothers. They probably both wanted the Typhoon with the chrome rims when the bikes were new; now the Hornet with the ivory-painted rims is more collectible.

Most boys' bikes of the 1960s were red, so a unique shade, like this candy gold, adds some extra rareness and desirability.

Bright candy purple paint, whitewalls, and a two-speed automatic hub help make this 1960s Schwinn Hollywood more collectible than the average girls' bike.

If you were fond of chrome, Sears had the model for you in 1963 and 1964. This virtually all-chrome 1964 Spaceliner is the deluxe "front springer" version.

When it came to Krate bikes, the striking Schwinn Sting-Ray Orange Krate was probably the top seller.

Up very near the top seller spot in 1971 was the red Sting-Ray Apple Krate.

Greg Bacha's 1971 Grey Ghost was one of the slower selling Krates in its day, but that makes it a bit more rare now.

Just when you think you've got something figured out, you don't. These Schwinn tandems are both 1963 vintage, but one is a "Twinn" and the other is a "Bicycle Built For Two." Note the variance in the front-chain tensioner positions.

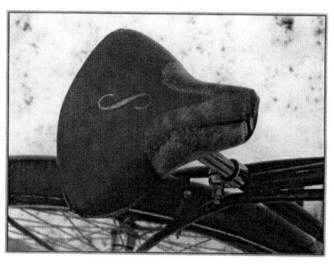

You can make seats like this one look new again by spraying them with aerosol flexible vinyl dye.

The white on this seat is almost as bright as the snow on the ground, after it was restored with flexible vinyl dye.

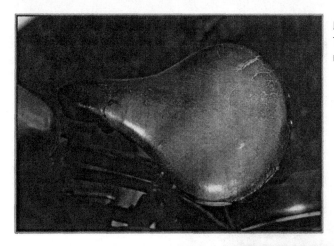

If original character excites you, look closely at old leather seats. The patina evident on the seat of Mike Carver's 1947 Whizzer rivals that of an antique baseball glove.

This thick leather Troxel seat is circa 1915. It must have been kept out of the weather, because the condition for its age is amazing.

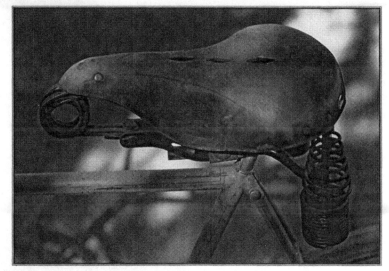

The yellow band automatics have a 1:1 second gear ratio, with a lower first gear.

Red-band hubs still have a 1:1 second gear, but have a different first gear ratio than the yellow band hub.

Blue-band hubs are actually overdrive units. They have a 1:1-ratio first gear and an overdrive-ratio second gear.

Speedometers add lots of fun to riding a bike, but if you ever hit 50 miles per hour, keep your eyes on the road.

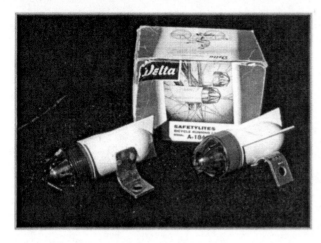

These Delta Safetylites add some nice color even when they aren't lit. They fit on the end of the front or rear axles.

Collecting head badges is a hobby all its own. Jerry Turner's display case shows off many rare badges, most of which he actually reproduced!

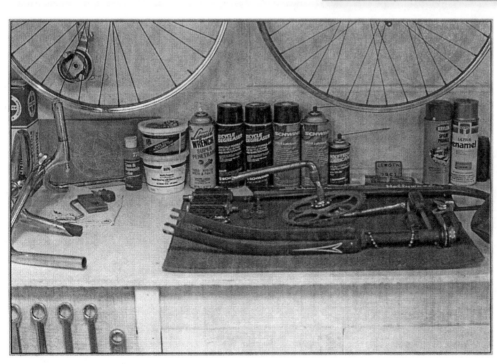

During restoration projects, work in a well-lit shop, with all of your parts and tools close by.

Don't be discouraged by surface rust on chrome parts, like this rim. As you can see, with some work, it will go away.

On his 1941 Monark Rocket, Dave added the tank, but painted and "aged" the tank to match the bike's original finish.

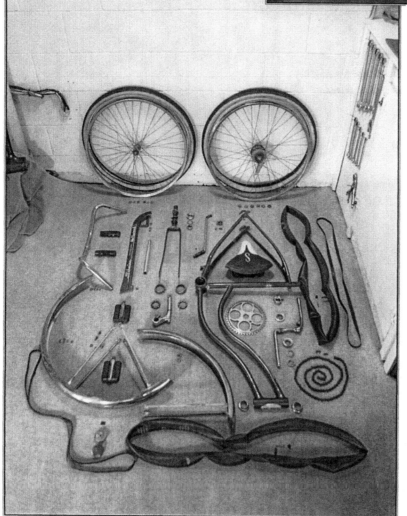

There are many parts to restore on a bicycle, but when you make each one of them the best it can be, the reassembled product is a sight to behold.

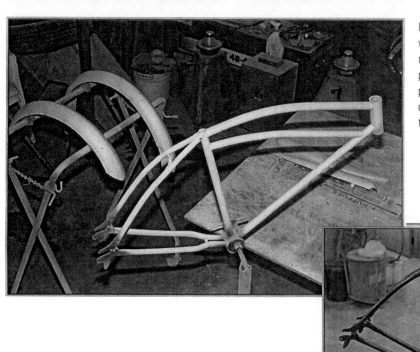

Here, the brown adhesion primer is visible where the lighter primer/surfacer wasn't needed. You don't want excess primer/surfacer where little sanding takes place. A build-up just increases the chance of chipping. Notice Eric's nifty jig for holding the frame during painting.

Eric wet-sanded the first coats of lacquer after they dried with 1,000-grit sandpaper. This helps the final coats of paint lay down smooth and flat.

Here is another one of Eric's great painting jigs. Now (using the proper respirator) he sprays the final gloss coats on the Hawthorne fenders.

Eric formed these fender chevrons using fine-line tape, masking, and spraying with vintage ivory. He used an old sales brochure to find the pattern.

Sometimes you can find a near-mint original bike like Jerry's 1951 J.C. Higgins gem with the original sales literature attached. Other times you may do a total restoration on something like the 1910 Iver-Johnson in the foreground. These are the extremes, but there are many conditions in between.

Observe the detail on Dave's 1941 Colson/Goodyear Clipper. He performed a concours quality restoration on this one, which includes a New Old Stock headlamp, computer-matched original color paint, and total replating.

Here's a full view of Dave Stromberger's rare, restored relic that could sell for a few thousand dollars. But after all that careful attention, would he really want to part with it?

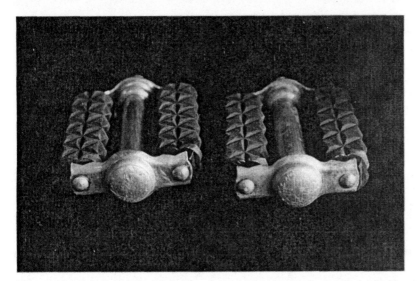

These pedal ends had no plating left, but the silver paint "trick" makes them quite acceptable.

Continued from page 64

Nuts, Bolts, and Screws

Don't neglect the restoration of small parts like nuts, bolts, and screws. If you have nuts and bolts that are rounded off, or screws with beat-up slots, look for replacements. Specialty suppliers and parts bikes are great sources. Rub bolt and screw heads, nuts, and washers with steel wool to restore their appearance. Use a flat file to clean up marks and burrs from nuts and bolts.

Keep Rubbing

As mentioned before, steel wool is one of your main tools of restoration. It's tedious, but rub each spoke to bring back its original, fresh appearance. Old spokes are cadmium plated and don't rust, but they *do* oxidize and corrode. Today, you have a choice for replacement spokes. These days not only are the cadmium-plated versions available but they also come in stainless-steel and chromed versions. Unless you're being a stickler for accuracy, try to use the newer versions. Old cadmium-plated spokes tend to be more brittle than their more modern chrome and stainless counterparts.

Use steel wool on anything that isn't painted, such as the seat post, seat clamp, coaster brake arm and bracket, and aluminum parts. The steel wool wears down and disintegrates as you rub, so it not only gets finer and finer, but you will also use it up quickly. Wax each part when your cleaning is complete to seal and protect it from oxidation and rust.

Painted Pieces

The main painted portions of your bicycle are the frame and fork but may also include fenders, rims, and accessories like a tank, rack, or light. If repainting is required, see chapter 7, but preserving an original finish is a growing trend. No matter how you approach this task, be sure to photograph every part of the frame so that if you eventually need to replace paint or graphics, you can come close to matching the original.

It is an unfortunate fact that some bikes have endured a bad repaint. If there is one coat or more of durable paint on your bike, stripping and repainting may be the only cure. Many bikes, however, have been brush painted with house paint. More than a few hobbyists have actually had success removing this kind

Wash all of your bicycle's painted pieces with any good soap and a wash mitt and/or brush. Stay away from super harsh cleaners, which can remove pinstriping or graphics. Do not use steel wool.

Surface scratches like the ones on this fork usually come off by rubbing with a polish or slightly abrasive compound.

There are many products to choose from, but a product with a medium abrasive works best. Rub the surface until oxidation and scratches go away. Don't remove any more of the surface layer than necessary, and finish up with a straight (non-abrasive) wax.

of paint to uncover an original finish. There are many products that are made for house paint removal, such as Kwikeeze by Savogran. There are some low-toxicity strippers manufactured by 3M that may take a bit more time to work, but are also a bit gentler on the paint that you are attempting to preserve. Experiment on small areas first to determine results. Even if you uncover most of the paint by this method, it takes a real feel for what you're doing to save graphics, pinstripes, or decals. At any rate, it's always better to have a marginal original finish than a bad repainted finish. You can always replace decals and pinstripes, but it depends on the condition of the original finish. New decals or pinstripes on an aged paint job don't blend in well. Good pinstripe artists can simulate old-looking pinstripes by thinning the paint, varying paint stroke pressure, and leaving breaks in the stripe.

The best situation is that your bicycle's original finish just suffers from dirt, oxidation, and some nicks and scratches. You can remedy all of these conditions to some degree.

First wash the pieces with an automotive wash soap or any cleaner like dishwashing liquid. You sure don't need to be concerned about saving any wax on the surface right now, but avoid harsh cleaners, which can remove thin pinstripes or silk-screened graphics. Dry everything with compressed air to get the moisture out of crevices and frame tubes.

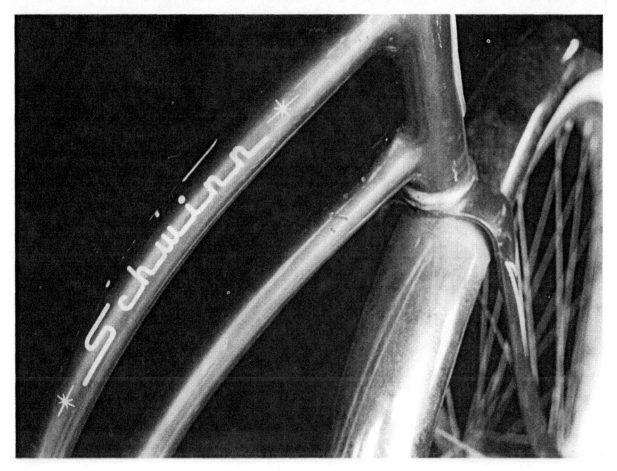

The nicks on this lower frame bar could use a brush touchup. Make sure the touchup paint matches, and place the paint only in the nick, not on the surrounding paint.

If any greasy dirt remains (like in the rear dropout area), use a solvent, thinner, or other degreaser and a small brush to dissolve it.

Now you can really see your paint. There is at least a thin layer of scratches and oxidation on the surface of the paint. There are also probably some nicks and scratches that are down to the primer or even to bare metal. Let's deal with the surface layer first.

There are more compounds, polishes, waxes, and "miracle" products available for paint treatment than you can imagine. Manufacturers' claims for results run the gamut as well. The practically senseless or maybe even superstitious use and reasons for recommendation of various products by individuals is nearly as endless.

Suffice it to say that to get off a dull layer of oxidized paint, you must use a polishing or rubbing compound with an abrasive (grit) of some type. These range from heavy to light grit; medium to light grit is the best choice for bicycles. There is a lot of painted surface on a bicycle's bars, so be patient. Rub the main color areas, being especially cautious around stripes and graphics. Rub just enough to remove the dull finish. Some surface scratches are deep into the paint, and others are just on the surface where some painted item has bumped the bike and deposited some of its paint. Rub a bit harder on spots where you encounter scratches. If you come across unwanted tape or stickers, warm them with a heat gun or hair dryer, then remove them. Use solvent to dissolve sticker "stickum."

After you've removed the oxidation and surface scratches, decide if you want to do some minor paint touchup. Brush touching every nick and scratch is not advised, as it will spoil the original look. If you are going to touch up anything, you need to find a matching paint. This process might be hit and miss, since

"Massage" out small fender dents from the inside, working against a block of wood.

caps on paints do not always match the color in the container, for example. Also, there is no paint "code" or name to reference, so you just have to look. Take a chain guard or fender into an auto paint store, or a hobby shop, and try to find a match. Sometimes, a metallic or unusual color is found in a nail polish, so you may have to take your fender into a cosmetics department. Certain auto paint stores use a computer to "read" your paint color and match it; give it a try if you can't find what you want elsewhere.

With paint touchup, be selective. Depending on how many defects there are, just paint the worst ones, and leave the others alone. You don't want a mottled look, since even

if the color matches, the texture will be visible. When painting, place the paint only in the nick or scratch, and not on the painted area surrounding it. This will minimize the sighting of the touchup. Touch up as many of the defects this way that seem right to you. Like other operations, the "feel" for the art of brush touchup will improve with practice.

Much of the pinstriping on old bikes is ivory or black; these colors are readily available. Touchup of pinstriping and graphics can look out of place if you are not careful. As mentioned, work in this area is sometimes "aged" with creativity. A piece like a rear rack or tank may also be repainted and distressed in some way, such as by rubbing the paint with a

rag before it dries, to blend it in with the look of the bike's other parts.

Massage out small dents in painted or chrome fenders with creatively picked tools of your choice. Auto body dollies are great, but the end of a screwdriver handle, a broom handle, a hammer, or some other device will work well too. A fender roller is a device (see picture in chapter 7) that rolls the fender between two rollers under pressure to remove dents completely. You must remove the braces to fully roll a fender, and find someone with a roller. You can buy one from classic bike specialists, but there's probably a collector in your area that has one; ask around, and you'll probably find someone to do it reasonably.

Scrub the tires with a stiff nylon or brass-bristled brush. It may take two or three repetitions to get off decades of accumulated filth.

Now after cleaning, rubbing, and touching up, wax everything with a straight wax (no abrasive) to protect your work. Set your painted pieces aside, and take a look at what's left.

Rubber Pieces

The tires and pedals are about the only visible rubber parts on your bicycle. There may be a bushing here or there on a spring fork, but they don't need much attention.

Good rubber cleaners are quite caustic, so wear rubber gloves while using these cleaners. An automotive tire cleaner like Westley's works nicely when accompanied with a brush and some elbow grease. Scrub the tires and pedals and rinse them clean. It may take two or three steps to get off all the old grime. When they are dry, you should have fresh-looking rubber pieces. Don't use rubber dressing unless your pieces have tuned gray or "chalky." Dressing lends sort of an artificial look to an old bicycle. If the rubber is very dry and cracked, look for replacements.

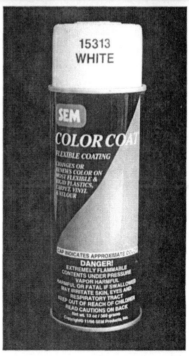

Vinyl seats with worn finishes can benefit from a touchup using a flexible aerosol coating like the one shown here.

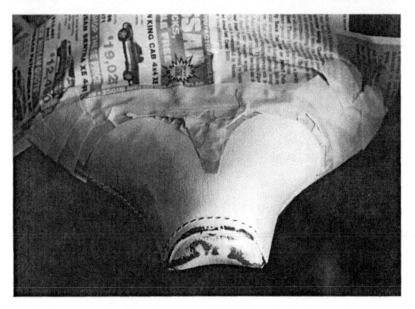
This seat has been scrubbed, dried, and taped to accept a new coat of white finish.

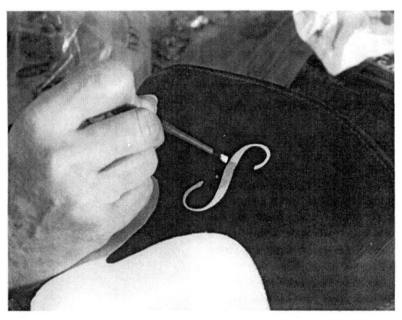
For small touchup, spray the aerosol paint into a small container (like the cap of the aerosol can), and apply the paint with a brush where you want it.

Seats

There isn't much you can do yourself with a worn-out leather seat, or for that matter, a torn or very worn vinyl seat. There are people in the business of recovering seats, however. Reproduction seats are best suited for total restorations, where everything looks brand new. A used seat that is better than the one you have is a good choice for an original bike.

Vinyl seats with worn finishes are very restorable. For this, buy flexible vinyl paint from an automotive paint store. These products are offered in a lot of colors and lay down an amazingly original-looking finish. Be certain to scrub and dry the seat surface totally before painting. Do not use regular paint for this purpose. Use masking tape to re-create patterns on two-tone seats. Touch up an "S" on a Schwinn seat by spraying a bit of the vinyl paint into a small container, like the paint lid, and apply the paint where needed with a small brush.

Head Badges

As mentioned elsewhere in this book, head badges present an entire area of collecting on their own. If yours is missing or badly damaged, you will be able to find one somewhere. One collector, Jerry Turner, actually reproduces head badges of every type, including a brass Chief badge with hand-inlaid porcelain.

Decals

In some cases, decals are sturdier than paint, while others come off during a wash job. Fortunately, a big number of decals are listed in classic bike supplier catalogs. Again, Jerry Turner, owner of Nostalgic Reflections in Veradale, Washington, will custom make any decal you need, in addition to offering many in stock

Some individuals collect bicycle head badges, and others even make them. Jerry Turner, of Nostalgic Reflections, can reproduce about anything, including this rare Chief head badge made of brass and porcelain glass inlay.

decals. Look for pictures shown in old sales brochures and advertisements to research decal types and positions for your bicycle.

Decals are sometimes used to replace silkscreen-painted graphics that have faded away (like on chain guards). Application of a decal requires a clean surface. Soak decals in water until you can slide them off of their backing. Put the decal in position, slide away the backing, and pat the area dry with a cotton towel.

Now that you've done about all you can mechanically and cosmetically to every part of your bicycle, it's about time to turn it back into a rideable machine. What are you doing right now? Let's put it together (chapter 8)!

Decals are available from several specialty suppliers. This one is for a mid-1950s Schwinn Corvette chain guard.

CHAPTER 7

Painting

Required Tools
Body dollies
Respirator
Latex gloves
Sandpaper (120, 150, 600,
     1,000, 1,500, and 2,000 grit)
Sanding pad
Paint, primers, sealer (see text
     and paint supplier)
Compressed air and paint gun
     (unless aerosol is used)
Body filler/glaze
Rubbing compound
Polish
Wax
Tack rags

Recommended Tools
Access to welders
Access to fender roller

If your restoration is to include a new coat of paint, you will either spend lots of time doing it yourself—or lots of money with a professional to achieve excellent results. Any shortcuts that you take in the preparation will be evident in the outcome. To duplicate the gloss and beauty of an original finish simply takes time. As discussed in chapter 3, if you do not wish to commit the time or money to paint your bike properly, keep the original finish. If the original finish is very bad, consider working with a different bike,

unless you're willing to paint it correctly. The main reason for this is that a substandard repaint will actually devalue your bike. A couple exceptions to this rule might be: cleaning up a kid's everyday bike or building a beach cruiser, where a fast "rattle can" spray job might suffice. To finish a nice collector bicycle, however, get ready for some work.

Your first step in the painting process is to remove all existing paint from the metal surface. The painted parts must be totally disassembled (chapter 4) and free of any attached

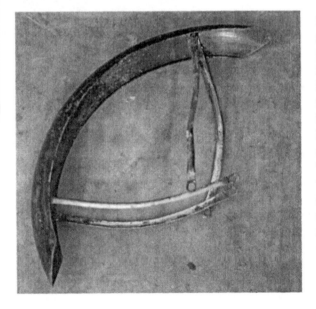

Disassemble all pieces to be painted. This includes removing braces from fenders, spokes from rims, horn buttons from tanks, etc. These 1938 Wards Hawthorne fender braces are supposed to be curved but not bent. Eric Christensen has some better braces from a parts bike donor.

hardware, such as bearing cups and brackets, before you begin any paint stripping. Remove spokes from rims, braces from fenders, and switches or buttons from tanks.

Chemical stripping is one option. The best variation of this is a commercial dipping process for paint and rust removal. This method works great, but unfortunately there are very few of these operations left in existence, due to environmental restrictions. If you are lucky enough to find one, simply hand over your rusty, painted parts to the dipper/stripper, and expect spotless, bare metal pieces when you return to pay the bill.

Chemical paint-stripping products are also available by the gallon from hardware outlets. For bicycles, these products are not preferable, due to their difficulty in removing original primer and inability to remove rust. These strippers are also very toxic to breathe and to touch. If you are familiar with their use and wish to try a home-use chemical stripper, you will still need to apply a rust-removal product before you paint.

Paint blasting has taken some new forms, mainly in the media used for the stripping process. This new bead-blasting technique relies on different blasting media: beads, glass, plastic, or acrylic material. They are designed mainly for polishing and stripping of softer metals, like aluminum. These newer materials will not warp large panels, either, but that's not much of a concern since there are no large panels on a bike. There is, however, usually some rust on an old bike, and these beads are not effective for rust removal. For bicycles, then, plain old sandblasting is the best bet, as it removes paint and rust very well.

Sandblasting is an available service in most areas, and unless you have

Find a professional sandblasting service in your area. They will have a commercial quality sandblaster unit like this one, ideal for stripping paint and rust from bicycle parts.

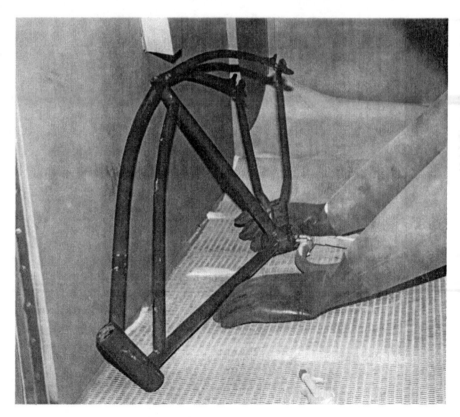

There is plenty of room inside of this unit for any bicycle frame. Note how the built-in gloves and sleeves isolate the operator from flying debris.

89

Christensen keeps a close eye on his work as he looks through the window of the well-lit sandblasting chamber.

access to the equipment to use your-self, go find a pro. Different shops will have varied opinions on the type of sand to use for the blasting process. The old standby is silica sand, in a preferred grain of about 70 grit, which will accomplish effective paint and rust removal. Disadvantages of this product are more for the opera-tor, including the ill effects of free sil-ica in the lungs, and the short life of the sand itself, which wears out rather quickly. Two other types of blasting

sand are copper and nickel slag. The copper slag is more angular and the nickel slag more round. Any of these kinds of sandblasting applied by a practiced user will effectively remove all paint and rust from your bicycle's frame, fenders, tank, fork, rims, and any other painted parts.

Once the parts needing paint are down to bare metal, inspect them closely for cracks, broken welds, or unwanted holes. Perform any metal repairs now. You must

get right on this, so you can prime the parts as soon as possible and avoid the onset of rust. You can do the welding on the frame or other parts only if you have experience with it. The best type of welding for frame cracks and repairs is the use of a flux-coated brass brazing rod, in conjunction with an oxy-gen/acetylene torch. If you cannot do the work, check with body shops, or even muffler shops, for this type of welding.

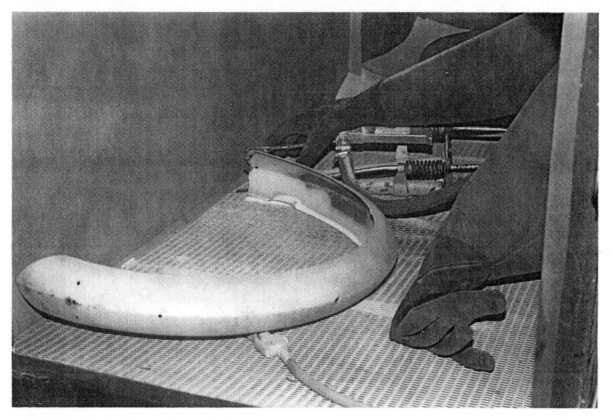

A proper sandblasting blasts just enough on any given area to remove rust and old paint. Excessive blasting can erode the surface of the parts. The stripped fender is now ready for priming, filling, and painting.

Unwanted holes in fenders or tanks are usually best repaired with a low-amp wire-feed welder. Any body shop has this type of welder on hand for use on thin metal. File or grind any type of weld as smooth as possible before filling, sanding, or priming.

Small dings, low spots, and filed-down welds are best filled with small amounts of plastic body filler. There are many brands available, but use a filler with a catalyst for quick setup. For bikes, since amounts of needed filler are minimal, a catalyzed glaze will usually serve your "filling" purposes. Follow product instructions for mixing, and use sparingly. Examples of filler use on a frame are repairing a hammer ding or feathering the edge of a weld. Remember, these frames and welds were not perfect

This frame is stripped down to bare metal so it can be inspected for cracks, broken welds, or unwanted holes.

Any weld should be filed or ground as smooth as possible before plastic filler and primer are applied.

from the factory. Remove any dings on fenders and tanks with body dollies or other tools, working the dents from both sides, against a block of wood to "massage" out the dents. For fenders, the very best straightener is a fender roller, made expressly for the purpose of dent removal. Ask around your town at bicycle shops, and you will probably find a hobbyist who owns a roller. If you plan to work on many bikes, a fender roller is a good investment; they work great for both chromed and painted fenders. Small amounts of filler may still be needed for low spots or pitting from rust.

After you sandblast, weld, grind, and fill, sand all parts lightly with medium (120–150)- grit sandpaper

prior to priming. Paint with a compressor and spray gun (modern guns are designated HVLP, or high volume, low pressure) if you can, or if not, purchase high-quality aerosol can products from an auto paint outlet. You have a choice of urethane, enamel, or lacquer paint for your final finish (pros and cons to be discussed shortly), but preparation and priming are the same for all paints. Consult with the people at your paint supply outlet for advice on paint application and compatibility. Use latex gloves while mixing paint, and use a respirator while spraying. Try to find a clean, well-ventilated area in which to apply your paint. Dust can stick to wet paint and it should be

sanded off before moving on to the next coat.

The primer you use on bare metal parts must be an adhesion primer. Types of adhesion primer are, for example, an epoxy primer like PPG D.P., or a self-etching primer available in aerosol. Spray only enough primer to evenly cover the surface. More is not better for primer application. If you apply too much primer, and get a thick buildup, it only increases the chance of chipping.

The adhesion primer is designed to form an excellent bond with the bare metal and provide the proper base for the next coat, which is primer/surfacer. For this coat, use a catalyzed primer like PPG K36 or a

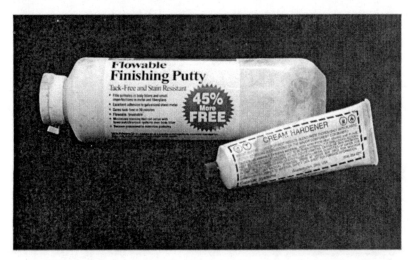

To fill and smooth small dings, low spots, and filed welds, use small amounts of catalyzed filler or glaze like the one shown here. Follow the manufacturer's instructions for mixing and application.

high-quality sandable primer in an aerosol can. As with the adhesion primer, spray sparingly, using only enough product to evenly cover the surface. You will be sanding this primer, so in areas that need little or no sanding, like the rear dropout area, it is not even necessary to apply the primer/surfacer.

After the catalyzed or sandable primer has set up, spray on a guide coat prior to sanding. This guide coat should be a darker contrasting shade compared to the sandable primer. Spray the guide coat in a speckled mist over the primer/surfacer. This guide coat enables you to clearly see low spots on the surface you are sanding. When sanding off the guide coat, the patterns you see will show you how smooth the surface really is. This allows you to make decisions on how many times to re-prime, or to even use additional small amounts of filler.

A 500-grit wet or dry sandpaper is ideal for sanding the primer and guide coat. This is where the main investment in time, through repeated sanding and re-priming, will pay off in the quality of the final paint finish.

Your own personal taste and desire for perfection will determine just how long you spend on this repetitious cycle of sanding, priming/guide coating, and re-sanding.

For the most efficient use of sandpaper, fold it once in half, then again in thirds. This will give you six sandpaper surfaces and also match the size of a standard rubber sanding pad. The rubber sanding pad should be about 1/4-inch thick, and be used for all primer sanding. If you don't use a pad, your fingers will follow the high and low spots, and leave no tell-tale pattern on your surface. Have handy a bottle of water to sprinkle or spray water continuously on the area you are sanding. Wet sanding provides more efficiency and keeps down the dust. Keep a cotton or paper towel nearby to wipe the surface and check your results. The high spots on your surface will show by getting to the original adhesion primer or the metal surface before the guide coat is off of the surrounding area. The guide coat will remain in the low spots. Use compressed air and a tack

Body hammers and dollies are useful for removing small dings in fenders and tanks.

The best way to make fenders look new is by "rolling" them. The fender roller shown here is a 1941 reproduction. A hobbyist or bicycle shop in your area probably has one. If you will restore many bikes, consider the investment.

rag to clean the surface before re-priming. After two or three steps of re-priming and sanding, the surface should be quite smooth. When you can sand off the guide coat without going through the sandable primer coat, you will have a very even surface. As with any hand operation, skill in sanding and "reading" the surface improves with practice.

When you like what you have for a base surface, rub it down with some wax/grease dissolver. Use a lint-free rag or paper shop towel for this. Now it is time to apply a light, even sealer coat. A product such as PPG Del Seal DAS or its equivalent works well. If you have some of your original epoxy primer or adhesion primer left (not the sandable primer/sur-facer), you can also use it for the

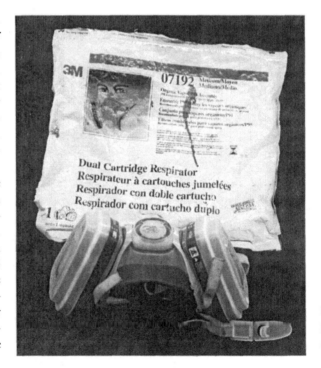

Use a proper respirator, like this one, for all painting.

Here Eric mists on a light guide coat of contrasting color, to aid in sanding. This speckled mist is sprayed directly over the sandable primer.

sealer coat. These sealers maximize adhesion for the final coat and minimize growth of surface flaws. Don't apply thick coats of sealer, or else spots called fisheyes (small spots of paint separation) might appear. If you have these spots, sand the surface with 600 grit, and re-seal with a couple of light coats. Depending on the sealer you use, it will be ready for paint in 30 minutes to 24 hours.

Finally, your project is ready for its crowning glory, the final paint application that is going to make all your work worthwhile. As noted before, you must choose whether to use urethane, enamel, or lacquer paint. Urethane paint is by far the most durable and is catalyzed for fast setup. However, it is the most toxic to breathe, takes experience to apply well, and has a gloss uncharacteristic of collector bicycles. Enamel is slower drying, hence more subject to gathering dirt and dust during setup. Lacquer is preferable for an amateur painter, due to its quick drying times and forgiving application properties. Lacquer is less subject to runs or an "orange peel" surface texture when compared to the other paint choices. Lacquer also buffs to a nice gloss, most duplicating a typical factory finish. Use a clear coat over metallic finishes to allow buffing without getting a blotchy finish. It will take between a pint and a quart of paint to fully finish a bicycle, so buy a quart to avoid running short or getting a remix that doesn't match. You will need 6 to 10 cans of aerosol for the job. Again, see your paint supplier for product advice.

With your paint chosen, place your parts in a bright area, so you'll have access to them from all sides. Hang parts, or build your own jig or racks, to give good access. Rub all

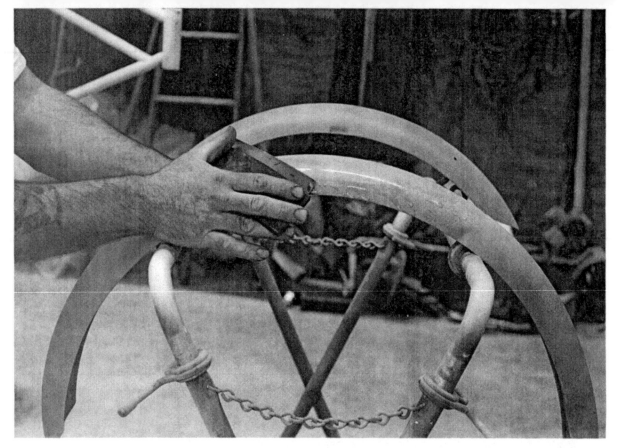

Use a sanding pad for primer/surfacer sanding. This will keep your fingers from following the high and low spots, and show you a telltale pattern on the surface.

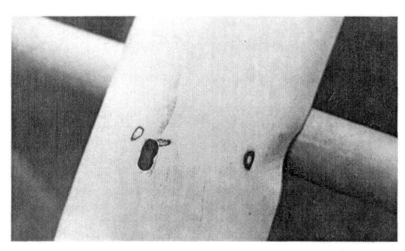

The telltale pattern of high and low spots shows up with light sanding. The rubbed-through spots (like the one to the upper left of the reflector hole) indicate high areas, and the remaining guide coat (above the hole) shows low areas. Repeated priming, guide coating, and sanding will create a very flat surface.

parts with a tack rag before spraying them with paint. A tack rag is a lint-free rag, available from your paint supplier.

Spray on about three light coats, as opposed to one heavy coat. Concentrate on even application; press and release your spray trigger before and after you pass your work, to avoid thick spots where strokes are started and finished. Lacquer requires only a few minutes between coats. Follow manufacturer/supplier recommendations in all cases.

After the paint is dry, you could polish the new surface and call it done. That is, you could—but don't. You've put in so much time already, wait about 24 hours and take a few

Here, Eric shoots inside of the fenders first, so they can dry and be placed on jigs for the outer coat.

more steps. To really make the result exceptional, lightly wet-sand the main surfaces with 1,000-grit wet or dry sandpaper and a sanding pad. This truly enhances the final outcome. When you spray with two or more final paint coats, you will notice how much more nicely they "lay down" than the first coats. Lacquer has another advantage here, because it sticks to itself recoat after recoat, even in unsanded areas. As a result, you only need to wet-sand the major surfaces, skipping areas like the rear dropout and the bottom bracket, which will still take paint

nicely. If you are recoating enamel or urethane after drying, all surfaces must be "roughed up" to accept more paint.

Your bike now has a beautiful finish, which is going to get downright gorgeous when you do the final rubbing and polishing. Unlimited products are available for the "buff and wax" routine, but again, your paint supplier will help you choose some that will work well. Wait 24 to 48 hours, depending on the paint product and temperature, before you do any rubbing. Actually, the rubbing process begins with sandpaper again.

Use 1,500- to 2,000-grit paper for a very light, final wet sanding.

Now is the time to add any painted-on graphics. Use fine-line and masking tape, available at paint outlets. Form and mask off patterns for fender chevrons, major pinstripes, or other designs. Make sure only areas where you want contrasting paint are exposed, and fully mask everything else with paper and tape. Spray on the contrasting color with two or three light coats. Small pinstripes and decals can be added later. When everything is fully dry and you have removed all the tape, wet-sand

97

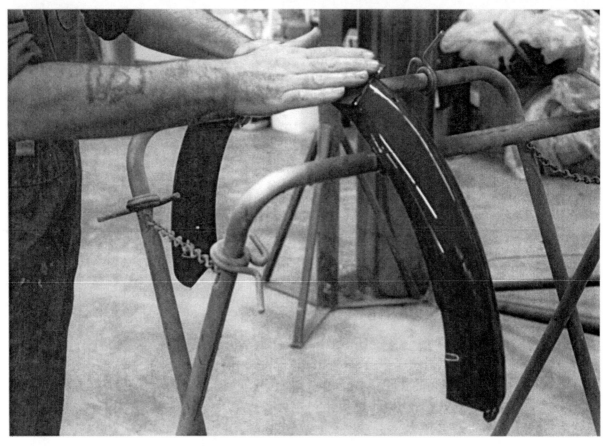

Here, Eric uses 1,000-grit wet or dry sandpaper to lightly scuff the surface one more time by wet sanding.

After wet sanding, the once-shiny fender is dulled again but super smooth.

lightly with 1,500- or 2,000-grit paper, especially the edges created by the tape.

Finally, get on to the rubbing and polishing. Use cotton towels or even the heavy-duty blue paper shop towels for this process. As mentioned before, there are many different products that will suit this purpose. Basically, this is a three-step operation: application of rubbing compound, polish, and glaze or wax. Buy a medium-coarse, all-purpose rubbing compound. The main tip for rubbing is to use the product sparingly, and rub lightly until the compound disappears from the surface. The "grit" in the compound wears smaller and smaller until it disappears, giving you

a graduated coarseness as you rub it away. One or two steps with the compound will eliminate all the fine lines (scratches) made with the 1,500- or 2,000-grit paper. Next, apply a polish, which is usually a combination of very fine grit or cleaner, and glaze, to get a really great shine. Simply wipe on the polish, allow it to dry, and buff it off with a clean cloth. Finalize your efforts with the application of a modern glaze (like Meguire's Final Inspection), a thin liquid product that smoothes the remaining micro-pores in the finish. A straight carnauba wax is wonderful protection also, but do not use it until about 30 days have passed, as it

The final coats of lacquer are evenly shot in two or three passes.

seals the surface too well for proper paint curing.

Pinstriping adorns many parts of some bicycles. These fine lines appear on bars, tanks, fenders, chain guards, carriers, and rims. Any pinstripes that you could not paint by tape and masking will need to be hand applied. Professional pinstripers can be found in regions all over the country, and in two words: find one. These artists have the special brushes, paints, and most importantly, the steady hand to lay down the lines any way you want them. Just make sure they know what you want before you let them loose on your bicycle. Sometimes they will take too much "artistic license" if left on their own.

Logos and lettering are often in the form of decals on collector bikes. Many collectors even replace original silkscreened graphics with duplicate decals. Sources are out there for most common decals, and there are artisans who will custom manufacture any decal. Ask someone in a bicycle club or a bicycle shop in your area for this kind of service. Chapter 10 lists sources for decals also.

When your bike needs painting, other parts often require plating or chroming. These other parts certainly need some restoration, if not replacement or re-chroming. Chapter 6 discusses cleaning and restoring these non-painted parts.

When all of the other pieces are ready, carefully put everything back together, using chapters 5 and 8 as your guide. You're going to get a lot of enjoyment and satisfaction as you combine all of your restored mechanical and plated parts with your newly painted pieces.

Finally, Eric is happy with these fenders, and later he will buff, polish, and wax them to a dazzling luster.

CHAPTER 8

Assembly

Required Tools

Wrenches, combination and
    adjustable
Pliers
Screwdrivers
Hammer and wood block
Hub wrenches
Valve stem tool
Lubricants
Goggles
Rags
Air source

Recommended Tools

Bicycle tire irons
Spanner wrench
Soft-faced hammer
Compressed air
Chain rivet tool
Kickstand tool
Vise
Bicycle stand
Sheet or tarp

By now, you've spent many hours with your bicycle through the disassembly and restoration process. You are very familiar with all of the parts, and should be well qualified to put the bike back together. Your assemblage of new, clean, or otherwise restored pieces will be easy and fun to work with. Reassembly is basically the reverse of disassembly. Gather your bags of small parts, along with the frame, fork, tires, rims, and accessories, and let's go!

Bearing Cups

As in disassembly, you need a starting point for reassembly. Begin by installing the crank-bearing cups in the bottom bracket, and the fork-bearing cups in the head tube. The left and right crank cups are identical, as are the top and bottom fork cups in most cases. This means you can't really put them in wrong.

Coat the surface of the cup that contacts the frame with a thin film of lubricant. An automotive engine assembly lube works well because it's thin and "clingy"; bearing grease works fine also. Now situate the frame on a wooden block (rag protected if you wish) so you can pound the tight-fitting bearing cup into place. Use your soft-faced hammer or a block of wood and a steel hammer to pound in all four cups (two for the crank and two for the fork). The main thing to check for here is that the lip which stops the cup from going in farther is fully seated to the frame. Check 360 degrees around the cups to be sure they are all the way in.

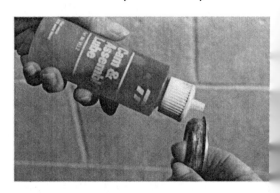

Coat the surfaces of the bearing cups that contact the frame with a thin film of lubricant. This automotive engine assembly lube works well because it's thin and "clingy." Bearing grease is okay too.

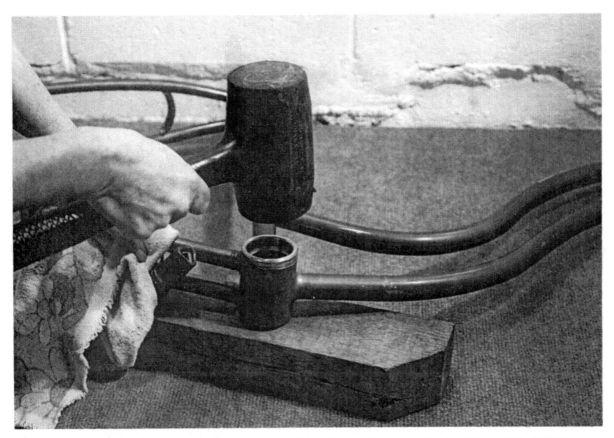

Place the bearing cup in the bottom bracket, and drive it in with a soft-faced hammer (or wood block and steel hammer). Check 360 degrees around the cup's lip to be certain that it is fully seated against the frame.

Pound all four cups (two crank and two fork) into position.

Tires

It's time to put your tires back on the rims. Start by placing the rim band (spoke nipple protector) on the rim. Locate the valve stem hole in the band, and align it with the hole in the rim. Stretch the band over the edge of the rim and into place. If you are reusing your bands, shift them slightly to get the spoke nipple indentations in their original spots. With a new rim band, just make sure it's centered on the nipples all the way around the rim.

Next, place the bead of one side of the tire only, fully onto the rim. Do this strictly by hand, as no tire irons or levers are need. Stuff the tube (valve core removed) into the tire, and over the edge of the rim, locating

Begin the tire installation by putting the rim band into position. Align the valve stem with the hole in the rim, and stretch the band slightly over the edge of the rim and into place.

First, place the bead of one side of the tire onto the rim by hand (no levers needed). Next, push the valve stem (from the inside) into the rim hole, and stuff the tube into the tire (with valve core removed).

the valve stem into the hole in the rim. Now push the remaining tire bead onto the rim, making certain that the tube is not pinched in the process. You may need a tire iron to pry the last part of the bead over the rim and into place; again be careful around the tube.

Add air from your compressor or floor pump to the tube. Hold the stem in place as you do this, so you don't push the stem back into the rim hole. **Caution:** Depending on your air source, it may only take four or five seconds to over-inflate and blow up a tire. Do this initial airing without the valve core in place, and only in one- or two-second blasts. Let the air come back out of the tube

Stretch the remaining bead over the rim's edge and into position, being careful not to pinch the tube.

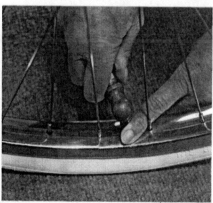

You may need a lever (screwdriver or tire iron) to pry the last portion of the bead up and over the rim's edge. Again, don't pinch the tube.

From your compressor or air tank, add air while holding the valve stem in place. Then the valve core should still be out, so you can let the air in and out a couple of times. Caution: It only takes air blasts of 2–4 seconds to fill a tire; don't blow it up!

between air blasts by removing the air supply chuck. This allows the tube to seat properly and lessens the chance of folds. Put the air in and let it out two or three times, then install the valve stem core. Again, if using a compressor, supply the air in one- or two-second bursts, checking the tire's pounds-per-square-inch (psi) of pressure with a reliable air gauge in between bursts. Most tires require 30 to 50 pounds (psi) of pressure; check the tire's sidewall for this specification. Screw on a valve cap, and repeat the process for the other tire.

Bearing Pre-load

It's time to consider something called bearing pre-load. This refers to the load, or pressure placed on a bearing set while it is at rest. It is your adjustment of the bearing cones that will determine pre-load. Pre-load can also be considered to be the tightness or looseness of a bearing system.

You will adjust the bearing pre-load on the crank, fork tube, hubs, and in some cases the pedals. Generally, tighten the adjustable cones just enough to remove the slack (checked as lateral, or side-to-side "wiggle"), and apply virtually zero pre-load to the bearings. You should err on the side of slightly loose, rather than tight, when adjusting bicycle bearings.

Fork Bearings

For the fork tube-bearing assembly, slide the bottom race (if you removed it) onto the fork in the proper direction. Now is the time to "dry test" the bearing fit by seating the bearings where they will ride, to be certain that they are not upside down. Test spin the bearings by hand against their respective cups and races (cones) to ensure proper placement and free rotation. If you have a photo record from disassembly, this will be easier.

103

After putting the fork and bearing assembly together, spin the upper cone on by turning it clockwise by hand. Tighten just enough to remove play or slack.

Pack the bearings and retainers with the proper bearing grease (see chapter 5: Bearing Lubrication). Apply a liberal coat to the cups and cones as well. It may seem basic, but be sure to install the fork in the correct end of the head tube (the bottom), as it will fit both ways but won't ride too well with the tire on top. Install the top-threaded bearing cone, washer, and nut to complete the assembly.

Hand-tighten the upper cone just enough to remove the slack. Rotate the fork a bit to even out the grease, then make a fine adjustment of the upper cone, which is usually knurled for a good finger grip. Adjust back and forth for too loose/too tight by trying to move the fork tongs side-to-side to determine slack, and rotating the fork to determine tightness. Again, tighten the cone just enough to remove clearance (slack), and no more. You will obtain a feel for this with experience. When the adjustment is just right, tighten the locknut while holding the adjusting cone in place. Use pliers, with a rag to protect the cone surface, and a wrench to fit the locknut, for this procedure. Rubber tubing can also be affixed to the pliers' jaws for protection. Because of the washer, you should be able to make a final snugging of the locknut without holding the cone, but watch the cone closely to see that it does not move, upsetting your adjustment. Wipe off excess grease with a rag, and you're done with the fork.

Crank Bearings

The procedure for installing the crank into the bottom bracket is similar to the fork installation. First, test-fit everything to confirm proper order and position of parts. If you didn't lube your bearings earlier after cleaning (chapter 5), pack them, and

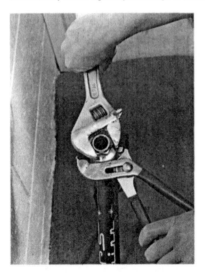

When the adjustment is just right, tighten the locknut while holding the adjusting cone. Here, the jaws of the groove joint pliers are fitted with rubber tubing to protect the adjusting cone.

The washer below the locknut should keep the cone from turning during final tightening. Use a hammer handle to hold the fork still while you tighten the locknut, and watch closely to see that the cone does not turn.

Lube the crank bearings, and apply a liberal coat of bearing grease to the bearing cups.

Remember, the crank threads are left-hand, so install and tighten the adjustable cone and locknut by turning them counterclockwise. Hold the cone still with your spanner wrench while tightening the locknut.

Perform the final tightening while holding the crank still with one hand and using the wrench with the other hand. In this photo, both hands push forward to tighten the nut. Be sure that the cone does not turn and upset the adjustment.

coat the cups and cones with grease. The crank/sprocket assembly will go in only a certain way. Usually, clearance is so crucial that if the bearing is in the cup, the crank won't go into the bottom bracket tube, for example. Dangle the sprocket side bearing on the crank, and position the sprocket away from the vertical frame tubes to install the crank. With the right position and a little patience, the crank assembly will go right in. You do not need to force the crank into the bottom bracket; if it binds, try a slightly different position.

With the crank seated in its bearing on the sprocket side, slide the remaining bearing in place on the other side, and install the threaded bearing cone, washer, and locknut. Remember from your disassembly, these are left-hand threads, so spin the cone and nut in a counterclockwise direction to install them. As with the fork, adjust the cone to remove slack, using your spanner wrench. Get the pre-load just right, then tighten the locknut, taking care that the adjustment is not changed. Make a final check by spinning the crank, and also testing for lateral movement. Readjust if necessary.

If you are using a bike stand, your bicycle is already stable. If not, now that the crank and fork are in place you can set the bike upright on a block of wood, such as a four by four, placed under the bottom bracket. Most hobbyists don't use bike stands, but those who do, love them. If you're working with a lot of bikes, they are worth the expense.

Hub Bearings

By now, you've got the bearing setup figured out: inner race (cup), bearings, outer race (adjustable cone), and locknut. Hub systems are about the same as the fork and crank setups,

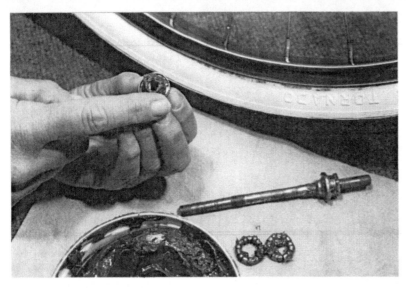

Pack the front hub bearings, and apply grease to the adjustable cones.

Apply bearing grease to the built-in front hub-bearing cups (races).

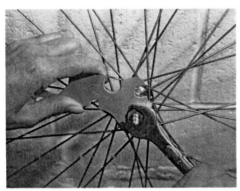

With everything in place, and with the bearing pre-load just right, tighten the axle locknut while holding the adjustable cone with a hub wrench. Apply clockwise pressure to the locknut, and counterclockwise pressure to the cone, to lock in position.

except that hubs have two adjustable cones and locknuts each, instead of one each for the fork and the crank. This is so the axle can be centered from left to right within the hub, or a front hub can be shifted to one side to accommodate something like a speedometer drive.

Again, test-fit the bearings for proper direction before final installation. For the front hub, pack the bearings and coat the built-in hub cups with grease. On hubs with loose balls (no ball retainers), place enough grease in the hub so you can stick the balls into position in the hub. Thread one cone onto the axle, leaving about an inch of axle thread showing on the outside of the cone. Place one bearing onto the axle, against the cone. Slide the axle into the hub until the bearing is seated in the hub, and test that it will spin freely. Place the remaining bearing into position on the opposite side, and thread its cone into place.

Now check for centering of the axle, and spin the locknuts up to the adjustable cones. Adjust bearing pre-load properly, and tighten the locknuts against the cones, while holding the cones with the appropriate hub wrench. Be careful not to change the adjustment during final tightening. Check for play or tightness, and readjust if necessary. Wipe off excess grease from the hub's exterior.

As written previously, rear hubs should be fully serviced either by a bicycle mechanic, or by you with the aid of an exploded diagram that shows internal parts. You can back off locknuts and adjustable cones to add lubricant and adjust side play, but be careful to hold the axle in place and not upset internal parts while doing this. A trace of side-to-side play at the rim is desired; over-tightening here will cause binding.

Handlebar Stem

Be certain that the long stem bolt is lubricated, and that the stem wedge threaded to it moves freely. Spin the stem bolt so that there is a slight clearance between the stem and the wedge. Also lubricate the wedge and the stem where they contact the inside of the fork tube. Slide the stem into the fork tube, and tighten the stem bolt, while keeping the stem aligned properly in relation to the fork. The stem height is adjustable up and down in the fork tube, and there is usually a maximum height mark on the stem. Never go beyond that mark—it's extremely unsafe to do so. For an initial adjustment, about midway between this mark and the lowest possible position is a good position. The stem bolt pulls the wedge into the stem as you tighten the bolt in a clockwise direction. This bolt needs to be pretty tight, but don't overdo it; excess torque on the long bolt can easily twist it into two pieces. After the handlebars and the front wheel are in place, you can test the adequacy of your tightening by holding the front wheel and trying to turn the handlebars left and right.

Be certain that both the long-stem bolt and the wedge threaded to it are lubricated and turning freely. Also lubricate the wedge and the stem where they contact the inside of the fork tube.

Handlebars

Simply slide the handlebars from either end into the stem, and center them. Personal preference will determine how you want to adjust the position of the handlebars. Placing the tips of the bar straight back, slightly downward, or even slightly

Slide the handlebars into the stem from either end, and center them. Up and down adjustment is a matter of personal preference. Tighten the clamp with the correct wrench when the bars are in the position you want.

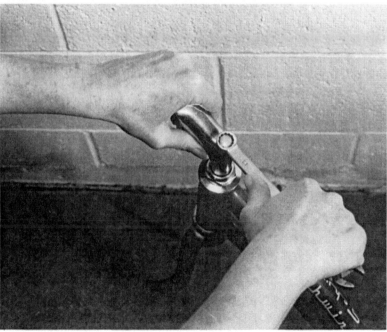

Tighten the stem bolt by turning it clockwise with the proper wrench, thereby pulling the wedge into the stem. This bolt needs to be pretty tight, but don't overdo it. Excess torque on this long bolt can twist it into two pieces.

upward are all acceptable. When you have them the way you like, tighten the stem clamp firmly. This clamp needs to be tight enough so you can't rotate the bars up or down and spoil your ride. But do not over-tighten this bolt, because doing so can result in a very unpleasant surprise as unexpected stress can then snap the bolt in the middle of a ride. Snug but not tight should be the rule of thumb.

Seat Post and Clamp

As noted in chapter 4, some bicycles have a removable clamp for the seat post, and others have a built-in clamp for a bolt and nut, or integral threads in the frame to accept a bolt. If you have a separate clamp,

With the handlebars and seat stem in place, the bike will sit upside down nicely. Here, a block of wood is placed under the seat stem to allow clearance for the rear fender installation.

For bikes with a built-in seat clamp, install the stem, bolt, nut, and washer, and tighten the clamp.

For bikes with removable seat clamps, slide the clamp in place before inserting the seat

slide it onto the frame tube so it is just below being flush with the top of the tube. On other types, simply lubricate the bolt, or the bolt and nut, and install them in the frame. Apply a very thin coat of lubricant of the bottom portion of the seat post, and slide it into the frame. Like the handlebar stem, position the seat post about in the middle of its positioning range for an initial adjustment, and tighten the clamp firmly. Whatever your seat height adjustment is, there should be at least 2 inches of stem within the frame.

Turn it Over Again

In preparation for the installation of the fenders, wheels, chain, chain guard, pedals, and kickstand, the bike should be turned upside down. With the handlebars and the seat post in place, the bicycle will sit nicely in this position. To make clearance for the rear fender, you may need to pace a block of wood under the seat post to raise the frame a bit.

Make sure that the handlebars are not directly in contact with a rough surface, like concrete. As in disassembly, use an old sheet or carpet under the bike to protect it. If you are using a bike stand, use the 360-degree rotation capability to turn the bike upside down for the next operations.

If your fender braces were removed for fender painting, dent rolling, or brace replacement, bolt rather than rivet them on. Specialty suppliers sell these short, smooth head screws. Some vintage bike suppliers even refer to them as "rivets."

Lubricate the threaded hole in the fork before you install the front fender and its screw.

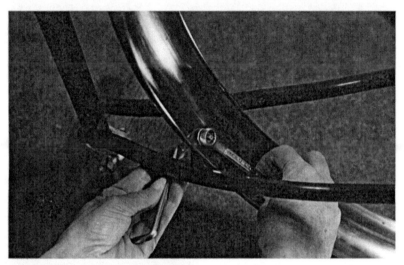

Fenders

If your fender braces were removed for fender painting, dent rolling, or replacement, bolt rather than rivet them back on. Some braces are screwed on originally, and in those cases, use original or original-type slotted screws. For once-riveted fender braces, a special screw is available that simulates a rivet (see photo). These short, smooth-headed screws have locking burrs under the heads, and are available from fastener suppliers and vintage bicycle parts outlets.

Fender installation is a very straightforward procedure. Hopefully, you have your fender mounting screws organized in bags, or marked in some way. Position the front fender, lubricate the screw that threads directly into the fork, and tighten it well. You can't get at this screw once the tire is in place, and you don't want the fender to rattle.

Place the rear fender in position, and attach it with the proper screws, washers, and nuts. One thing to pay attention to is visible screw slot alignment. Since you're trying to make the bike look as good as it can be, aligning your screw symmetrically is best. You can align them side-to-side, fore-and-aft, or up and down. It's your choice, but don't just leave them in

Above: It's easiest to hold the fender screw and turn the nut with a wrench. Here, the "L"-shaped screwdriver is used because of limited clearance.

Left: For a good look of detail, align screw slots symmetrically. For example here, align the slot fore and aft, or side to side. A random position doesn't look as good.

Right: To align a screw the way you want, hold the screw in position with a screwdriver, and do the final tightening by turning the nut with a wrench.

109

Attach the fender braces, nuts, washers, and other hardware in the proper order before tightening the axle nuts.

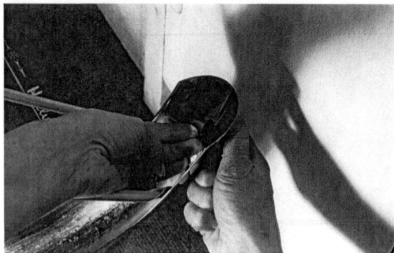

Attach the rear reflector before installing the rear wheel. It's hard to get at the reflector attachment hardware with the wheel in place.

random positions. To achieve this, hold the screw slot in the desired position, and do the final tightening to the adjoining nut with a wrench. This is a small detail, but aesthetically improves the overall look. This same principle should be applied to bolt heads and nuts also.

Front Wheel

Next, position the front wheel into the fork tongs (front dropout). One note about tire positions: the rear wheel can only go in one way because of the sprocket. If your tire sidewall markings are different on each side, position the front wheel, which can go in either way, so that the tire markings match those of the rear tire. Seat the axle fully in the dropout slots, and place any fender braces, fork arms or truss rods, carrier braces, and washers over the axle ends. As mentioned in chapter 4, a photo record of the order of placement of these items is helpful now. Install the axle nuts and tighten them both in a clockwise direction.

Rear Wheel

It's time to install the rear wheel, but first attach the rear fender reflector, since it's easier to get to the inner

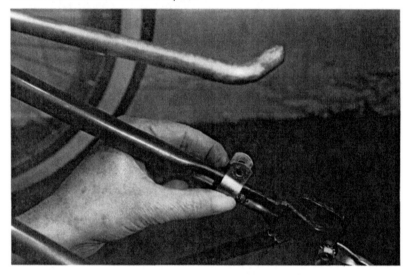

For coaster brake models, slide the brake arm bracket onto the frame. Install it at the narrow area near the rear dropout, and slide it into position.

fender mounting hardware with the tire out of the way. Also for the common coaster brake models, slide the brake arm clamp onto the frame. To avoid scratching the paint, install the clamp at the thinnest part of the frame (close to the rear dropout), and then slide it into its final location. Place the rear-wheel assembly into the dropouts, and loose-fit the washers

and nuts by hand. Also align and loose-fit the coaster brake arm to its bracket. Do not tighten any of these nuts until the chain is installed and adjusted.

Chain

If you haven't lubricated the chain yet, either work bearing grease into it with a rag, or spray on a quality

Lubricate the chain by rubbing it with bearing grease as shown, or by spraying it with a product designated for bicycle chains.

While adjusting the chain (moving rear axle in the dropout slots), you must also center the wheel between the lower frame rails.

chain lube before installation. Put a very small amount of grease on the teeth of the front and rear sprockets as well. After servicing your chain (chapter 5), it should bend freely at all of the rivet positions. If your chain is tight at any of the rivets, or it is still rusty, consider getting a different one. It's no fun to apply power to the pedals of your new ride, and have the chain slip, or worse, break.

Place the chain over the sprockets, install the master link, and snap the master link cover into its locking grooves. If you have no master link, install the joining link with your chain rivet tool (chapter 5 photos show detail). Next, properly adjust the chain tension, a procedure that is highly important. While adjusting the chain, you must also center the wheel between the frame rails, which extend from the bottom bracket.

As a chain assembly is rotated, there will be tight and loose sections. Rotate the chain until you find the tightest spot between the sprockets. The chain slack at this point must be 3/8 to 1/2 inch (see photo). If the chain is too loose, you'll get the dreaded chain-to-chain guard rattle on bumps. If the chain is too tight,

Chain tension is important, and 3/8- to 1/2-inch slack, when checked at a point midway between the sprockets, is proper.

111

Some of the very old bikes have chain adjustment screws, like motorcycles. This feature disappeared sometime in the 1940s.

you will have hub binding, unwanted noise, or grinding while driving. An overly tensioned drive chain adversely affects the rear hub operation for certain. When everything feels right, tighten the rear axle nuts in a clockwise direction, and tighten the coaster brake arm clamp.

For derailleur models, the chain is self-adjusting to a degree. The chain length is the crucial factor, and must be long enough to go around the front sprocket and the largest rear sprocket, without bending the derailleur arm fully forward. A chain that is too long will hang loose when it is on the smallest sprockets. Derailleur hubs are not present on most collector bicycles but do appear on muscle-type bikes. As with all types of rear hubs, and as mentioned elsewhere, disassembly and repair or service of rear hubs might require a professional bicycle mechanic's assistance. If you do want to work on any certain rear hub, try to obtain a manual, or at least an exploded diagram specific to your hub. Internet auctions, hobbyists, bicycle shops, and parts suppliers are sources for this information.

Chain Guard

Some very old bikes don't have chain guards by design, but if your

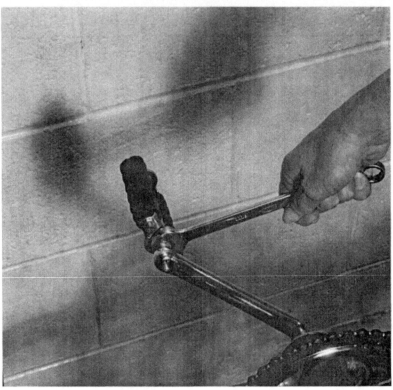

Thread the pedals onto the crank arms, remembering that the left-hand pedal has a left-hand thread. In this picture, the wrench is pushed downward to tighten the pedal.

bike has a chain guard, install it now. On models with a clamp-type rear attachment, use caution not to scratch the paint when placing the clamp over the frame. If there is a built-in frame-mounting tab at the front, it is possible to position the chain guard's front bracket to the left or right of this tab. The correct position is the one that most centers the guard over the chain and does not interfere with the crank. Install and tighten the screws.

Pedals

Your parts bags should just about all be empty at this point. Now screw the pedals back in, remembering something learned during disassembly. The left-hand side of the bike (looking down, from a riding position) has a left-hand

threaded pedal. While viewing the bike upside down, this can get confusing, but there is an easy way to figure it out. Per chapter 4's information, you remove the pedals by turning the wrench in the direction that applies the coaster brake (backward). This works for both pedals and with the bike in any position. Now install both pedals by inserting them, and tuning the pedal shaft in the direction that rotates the crank forward. In this case, you must hold the crank still in some way, as you do a final tightening on the threaded pedal shaft. If the pedals do not thread-in readily by hand, they are probably reversed. Pedals are generally marked "L" or "R" at the inside end of the axle shaft. Whatever you do, don't try to force a pedal into the wrong side with a wrench.

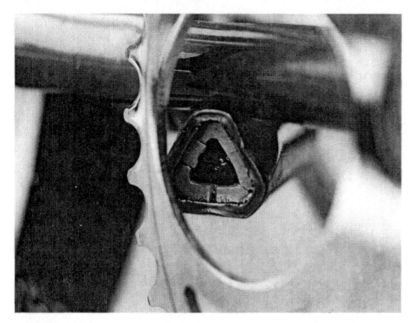

If you took out your kickstand position cam, be sure to reinstall it with the slash mark toward the bottom of the bike.

Kickstand

Install you kickstand now, so you can turn you bicycle over and admire it. The bolt-on types, whether the swing arm, or single lever–type, are simple to bolt on, so go ahead and do it.

If you have the built-in Schwinn type, and you took it out (chapter 4), then you know something about installation already. Be certain that the positioning cam is placed properly in the frame tube (the mark on the side of the cam that points to the sprocket denotes the bottom), and that the spring and its keeper are in place. Lubricate the spring and the keeper with bearing grease. Install the sprag assembly into the frame tube, and push the grooved collar (with a special tool, or as described

At a midrange setting, the top of the seat should be in line with the handlebar stem bolt (with the handlebar stem at a mid-setting). They should be moved up or down as a pair to accommodate a rider's size.

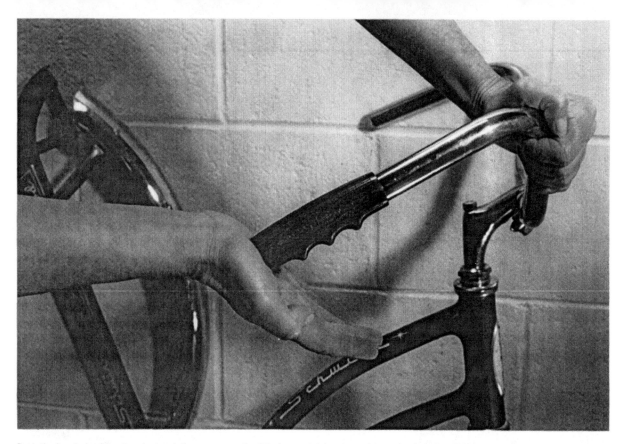

Push the handgrips into place by hand. If necessary, a tiny bit of spray lubricant may be used to help install tight grips. Never use glue!

in chapter 4) far enough into the tube to drop the large end of the retaining pin into the hole in the frame tube. When the pin is fully seated, release the tension on the collar, and the pin will stay in place.

Finally, it's time to set your project back on its wheels. Turn the bike over, and make sure the kickstand is down and working before you let go of it. If you have brand-new paint, you'll be especially sad if you tip it over now.

Seat

Position the seat by placing the seat attachment bale over the stem. On many models, the bale can be rotated to a fore or aft position, to adjust the seat to a more forward or a more rearward position. The rearward

position (bale rotated to the front of the seat) is considered the standard setting. A forward seat position (bale rotated to the rear of the seat) is for smaller riders. The seat height is also determined by the rider's size. A standard setting is about midrange, with the front of the seat pointed to the stem bolt (see photo), with the stem at a middle setting. Level the seat (viewed from the side), line it up fore and aft, and then tighten the seat clamp (bale). Muscle-bike seats employ a stem up front, and attach at the rear along with the fender braces or at the rear axle.

Handgrips

Now the easiest is left for last. Right where you began disassembly,

Don't roll your bicycle around without air in the tires. This is why you see crooked valve stems. Bring the air source to the bike, or carry the bike to an air source before rolling or riding it.

Your hard work has now paid off, as you have restored the beauty of, and brought new life into your prized collector bicycle. Now, take it for a test ride!

you are going to finish up. Install the handgrips on your re-plated or otherwise restored handlebars. This really should go easy, with a simple push or twist. Remember, don't use glue, and in fact, a small amount of spray lube is good to use if the grips are especially tight going on.

One Last Tip

Bicycle tires tend to lose air while sitting. Do not roll your bicycle around without sufficient air in the tires. If you must move your bike to an air source, pick it up. Rolling on empty tires causes the valve stems to become cocked, and eventually will damage the tube. If you are rolling your bike around, or riding it, make sure there is adequate air in the tires.

Way to Go

Congratulations—you've made it through a bicycle restoration; buff off the handprints and admire! Don't look at the flaws; you are more aware of them than anyone else. Your project may have been a total repaint and restoration; a simpler clean, repair, and restoration; or one of the many classifications within that spectrum. No doubt, you've learned a lot and have enjoyed both the process and outcome. If this is your first restoration, you'll most likely restore another. If you took on a lesser project this time, you may want a bigger challenge next time; if you just finished a total repaint, you may find a bicycle with paint you can reuse next time.

Wherever you take the bicycle collecting and restoring hobby, you will be among many others who enjoy the same thing.

The following two chapters cover other fun parts of the hobby. Personalizing your bicycle with accessories is popular and easy. For more serious personalizing or customizing, there are no boundaries, and many hobbyists prove this.

To obtain stock parts and custom accessories, parts sources and clubs are available. Some hobbyists believe that the "treasure hunt" required to gather parts for an old bike is the most enjoyable aspect of the hobby. Don't worry—clubs and swap meets will always be around to demonstrate that you are not the only one afflicted with the "bicycle bug."

CHAPTER 9

Accessories

Do you want to give your collector bicycle a personal touch? Accessories are available in seemingly endless varieties. As a general rule, you should install accessories from the same era as your bike. Rules are made to be broken sometimes, as you'll see in a bit, with Jim's 1959 custom Corvette "hot rod."

Lights are either battery or generator powered. Most collectors leave the batteries out of the lights, except for special occasions. The

Here's a hefty light, more like a lantern, atop the fender of a 1941 Colson/Goodyear Clipper.

One novel approach to a headlight is this vintage flashlight holder.

Lights are either battery or generator powered, except for antique gas-powered lamps.

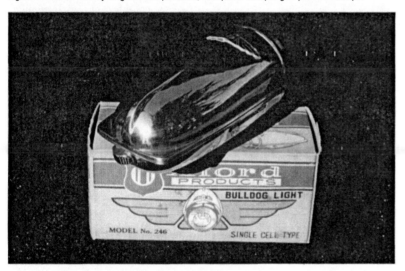

It's nice to find NOS (New Old Stock) accessories like this Oxford light with tail fins.

Many speedometers are manufactured with the bicycle maker's brand name imprinted on their faces, like J.C. Higgins.

This speedo face not only has the brand but the model name as well (it's worth a lot).

batteries rattle and eventually leak. Very early lamps are actually gas or kerosene powered, and appear only on true antiques from the turn of the century.

Radios are found in the form of transistor models popular in the 1960s. These are battery operated, and some of them even combine a radio with a headlight.

Horns are manually operated (bulb or bellows) or battery equipped.

There are so many types of horns that a collecting hobby of horns alone is common. Some warning devices are bells, which seem to have a timeless popularity.

Speedometers for collector bikes are generally combined with odometers and are cable driven. They run off of the front wheel and must match the wheel diameter (20, 24, or 26 inch) for accurate operation. One of the

rarest versions is the Sting-Ray–designated model from Schwinn.

Turn signals were offered for just about every make of bicycle, and you could also buy generic signal kits from outlets like Sears and Western Auto.

Streamers were probably installed at least once by all of us. They are cheap, available almost everywhere, and can be installed in a few seconds. To put them on, just poke the spring that is

Turn signals are a popular accessory, another example of the bicycle/auto association.

you'll have to drill a hole to mount it.

Reflectors are custom mounted on almost any portion of a bicycle one chooses. You have a variety of types and sizes to pick from, and mounting methods and positions are totally up to you. Besides the typical rear fender location, reflectors are seen on frames, pedals, chain guards, spokes, baskets, racks, mud flaps, and just about anywhere else.

Racks are one of the accessories you will select for function as well as looks. Officially designed for holding books, you can strap a variety of cargo to a standard rack, or even squash a few things in the spring-type models.

Baskets are functional like racks but hold even more cargo. They mount on the front handlebars or over the front or rear fenders in saddlebag fashion.

Hub shiners are small strips of leather that you secure around

Mud flaps come in many varieties. These, with molded-in checkered flags and a reflector, are 1960s vintage.

attached to the streamer into the handgrip hole.

Mud flaps are found in brand name and generic models. You can mount a rear mud flap to the reflector shaft inside of the fender. Make sure you want a mud flap on the front fender before you install it, because

Jeweled reflectors are popular, and the back of a rear rack is a common place to find them.

Hub shiners add a bit of style, and clean the hubs as you ride. Schwinn makes beautiful reproductions of their originals.

Custom handgrip and seat choices are strictly up to your own tastes. As with so many other accessories, varieties are many, but choose one that matches the era of your bike for the best look.

Custom valve caps are available in about any form that you can think of. Like streamers, they are popular because of their wide availability and ease of installation.

the front or rear hubs. They rub off and absorb grease and dirt automatically as the bike moves. Schwinn produces excellent copies of those originally used on many of their early bikes.

Tanks range from simple decorative designs to deluxe models with louvers, lights, and horns. You can upgrade a basic-model bicycle with a tank from a model that is higher in the lineup of the same brand. Different brands sometimes interchange also, which pleases the customizers.

This sturdy, fully chromed rear rack has fins built in at the back.

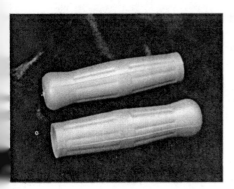

Custom handgrips, like these "Coke Bottle" beauties, come in many shapes and colors.

paint finish, because this bike is ridden a lot (over 7,000 miles so far), and high durability is needed.

The Phantom tank is a 1950 original (reproduction units are currently available from Schwinn dealers) with new paint. Besides the tank, the Schwinn front carrier, and the 1962 Corvette II chain guard, the remainder of custom pieces consists of a real mix of manufacturers.

These accessories and replacement pieces are some of the best available from around the globe. Once again, Jim really rides this bike a lot; he regularly heads out on 50- to 100-mile road trips, and needs to keep up with the newer road bikes that he rides among. To do this, Jim feels he needs the following list of goodies: Minoura dual water bottle carrier, Elite ST rear sealed-bearing six-speed derailleur hub, Elite VT sealed-bearing front hub, sealed-bearing

Jim Houghton doesn't ride his custom hot rod in the snow, but with over 7,000 miles logged, snow is about all that stops him.

Jim's Hot Rod Corvette

Jim Houghton has taken parts and accessories from current bike technology, and tastefully and functionally blended them into his hot rod Schwinn Corvette. This 1959, 26- inch boys' model has the classic cantilever frame, which is a very solid base for a custom rider.

After the frame was down to bare metal, Houghton welded on some custom pieces to accommodate the derailleur hub and various cables. Next, he applied a heavy gray urethane

There are many new style, specialized parts here, even though the overall look is vintage.

trendy low rider customs. If you like to be creative, there are no limits. Many independent bicycle shops and franchised dealers around the country get creative with custom bikes. The folks at Columbia Cycle and Hobby in Spokane, Washington, enjoy making these creations, for example. Check with bike shops in your area for help, if customs interest you. Many brands now offer factory custom cruisers to satisfy the recent popularity and demand for these fun bicycles.

The slick-tread Avocet FasGrip City tires hold 80 to 100 psi of air pressure for low-rolling resistance.

Sealed crank bearings in the bottom bracket minimize friction and maximize longevity.

Takagi CR-MO crank, Specialized SP 150 pedals, Araya RM 20 rims, Avocet Fas-Grip city tires, Shimano shifter/derailleur, Dia-Comp brake levers, Brooks Champion B66 seat, and a Vetta speedometer/timer.

Bicycles are versatile for customizing because of parts interchangeability between different years and brands. Hobbyists love to compile and assemble their own creations; the old frames are even modified and used as bases for the

CHAPTER 10

Resources

Bicycle restoration requires the availability of replacement parts. Unless your bike is 100 percent complete, you will need some parts. Fortunately, the hobby is strong enough to support specialty vintage parts suppliers. These businesses gather and sell used, reproduction, and new old stock (vintage unused) bicycle parts. Some of the popular vintage suppliers are listed at the end of this chapter.

Many bicycle shops that sell mainly new bicycles also have a collector bicycle sideline. One such bicycle dealer is Columbia Cycle and Hobby in Spokane, Washington. Ask around in your area, and you will most likely find a shop, or at least an employee in a shop, who deals with old bikes.

Swap meets are held throughout the country, the largest being the annual one in Trexlertown, Pennsylvania. This

Bikes that are useful as parts donors are found in bicycle junkyards and thrift stores. This location seems to have everything but the kitchen sink—although it does have a bathroom sink.

Hobbyists' basements and garages can hold a wealth of desirable parts. This garage has several fairly complete bikes.

This collector's basement houses a great supply of parts, which are even kind of organized.

Need some whitewalls? Look no further, but you better have some parts to trade. Most collectors prefer getting parts instead of money for their wares.

the one that you are restoring but have many parts that will fit your bike, such as kickstand parts, sprockets, cranks, handlebars, bearing sets, and fender braces, just to name a few.

If you're building a custom bike, for example, you may want a Sturmey Archer cable-operated three-speed rear hub with a coaster brake, which was offered in 1978. This is a great three-speed to use on an old bike, because hand brakes are not required. Earlier Sturmey Archer three-speed hubs have no coaster brake feature. The newer three-speed with the coaster brake version has a typical 36-hole spoke specification, and you can lace it to any old 36-hole rim. You can purchase an old bike in rough shape with this hub for next to nothing.

Research what you are looking for, so you don't end up buying parts you can't use. As an example, forks for 24-inch versus 26-inch bicycles are slightly different in size. They look about the same, but you must

A bike that is donating parts can be much newer than the bike in need of the parts. Fork bearings and cups from this late-1970s Schwinn will fit bikes back to the 1950s.

is a real bicycle town, complete with a velodrome (indoor bicycle track); their event is held on the first Sunday in October. Vintage auto swap meets usually have a couple bicycle vendors in attendance also.

Among existing bicycles, condition runs from top to bottom. Those in the bottom category make great parts donors. These bikes are found in bicycle junkyards, thrift stores, bicycle shops, hobbyists' garages, yard sales, and many other locations. Parts bikes are a great source for just about anything, and a bike in horrible condition may still have usable bolts, screws, nuts, washers, bearings, etc. A parts bike can be much newer than measure them to make a positive identification. Bearings must be matched up with their cups and cones to ensure interchangeability also. Front sprockets may look similar, but count the teeth. A 52-tooth front sprocket makes it harder to pedal than a 46-tooth version. A couple different chain types will be encountered as well. Bicycles have very interchangeable parts, but make sure you check out possible differences before using parts taken from different bikes.

It is hard to find a national bicycle club, but many local ones do exist. The next best thing, however, is the Internet. There are more vintage-related websites on the Internet than you can explore in a lifetime. Discussion forums, bikes for sale, parts for sale, and individual hobbyist websites are abundant, to say the least. Use the photo archives at many of these sites to research what you need.

Speaking of websites, Internet on-line auction sites, like eBay, have rapidly become a top source for bikes and parts. If you are patient and persistent, you will find what you want, and learn more about your bike as you do.

Listed here are some tested organizations that are good resources for your project, from start to finish. Each one of them can contribute in some way.

The Eastwood Company
263 Shoemaker Road
Pottstown, PA
(800) 345-1178
(610) 323-2200
www.eastwoodco.com
Restoration tools and supplies

Memory Lane Classics
24516 Third Street
Grand Rapids, OH
(419) 832-3040
www.memorylane-classics.com
Vintage bicycles and parts

Maple Island Sales
59 SW 5th Lane
Lamar, MO
(417) 682-6655

www.mapleislandsales.com

Vintage bicycles and parts

Menotomy Vintage Bicycles
P.O. Box 2864
Acton, MA
www.oldroads.com
Vintage bicycles and parts; hub diagrams; serial number charts

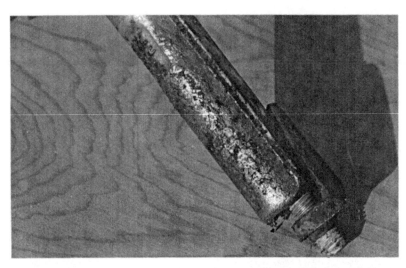

A handlebar stem is another item that can come from a newer bike, where the wedge is not frozen to the bolt.

The kickstand positioning cam (behind the sprocket) can be taken out of this 1978 model and placed in a 1958 model.

This unusual rear hub is a cable operated three-speed unit with a coaster brake. It could make a nice custom hub for an old bike, because it doesn't require handbrakes. The missing screws have already been transferred to another bike.

Some front sprockets may look interchangeable, but you should count the teeth before swapping. More teeth make the bike harder to pedal.

Vintage Tire Hotline
1-800-251-6336
http://www.coker.com
Vintage and reproduction tires

Schwinn Factory Page
Vintage collector and restoration
forums
www.schwinnbike.com

eBay Auction
On-line auction with bicycle and parts
categories

Dave's Vintage Bicycles
Davenport, WA
www.nostalgic.net
Vintage Bicycle Expert

Nostalgic Reflections
P.O. Box 350
Veradale, WA
(509) 226-3522
Vintage decals and head badges

Rainbow Cycle Craft
201 Murray St.
P.O. Box 180
Niwot, CO 80544
(303) 652-2424
Bicycle paints and decals

Trexlertown Swap Meet
First Sunday in October
Trexlertown, PA
(570) 275-1166

Park Tool
6 Long Lake Rd.
St. Paul, MN 55115
(651) 777-6868
http://www.parktool.com
Specialized tools for bicycle mainte-
nance and restoration

BikeIcons
256 Lincoln St.
Saco, ME
Vintage bikes and great links to other
websites

Coker Tire
1317 Chestnut Street
Chattanooga, TN 37402

Other swap meets annually occur in Butler, Pennsylvania; Swansea, Massachusetts; Boston, Massachusetts; Fresno, California; Buffalo, New York; and Long Beach, California. Check local clubs and websites for dates. Remember—one of your local bicycle shops probably has a collector bicycle buff on staff, so check it out!

SHOP NOTES

INDEX

LaVergne, TN USA
09 December 2009
166465LV00003B/29/P